.MURDEROUS **MATHS**.

Murderous Maths

More Murderous Maths

The Essential Arithmetricks
How to + − × =

The Mean and Vulgar Bits
Fractions and Averages

Desperate Measures
Length, Area and Volume

Do You Feel Lucky?
The Secret of Probability

Vicious Circles
and other Savage Shapes

JOIN THE MURDEROUS MATHS GANG
FOR MORE FUN, GAMES AND TIPS AT
www.murderousmaths.co.uk

Also by Kjartan Poskitt:
The Knowledge: The Gobsmacking Galaxy
Dead Famous: Isaac Newton and his Apple

MURDEROUS MATHS

KJARTAN POSKITT

Illustrated by
Trevor Dunton

Scholastic Children's Books
Euston House, 24 Eversholt Street,
London NW1 1DB, UK
a division of Scholastic Limited
London ~ New York ~ Toronto ~ Sydney ~ Auckland
Mexico City ~ New Delhi ~ Hong Kong

Published in this edition by Scholastic Ltd 1999
First published in the UK by Scholastic Ltd 1997

Text copyright © Kjartan Poskitt 1997
Cover illustrations copyright © Philip Reeve 1997
Inside illustrations copyright © Trevor Dunton 1997

10 digit ISBN 0 439 01156 6
13 digit ISBN 978 0439 01156 3

Typeset by TW Typesetting, Midsomer Norton, Avon
Printed and bound by Bookmarque Ltd, Croydon, Surrey

18 20 19 17

Contents

Murderous maths – are you kidding?   7

The basics   12

Professor Fiendish's fatal fungus   19

The best invention ever!   27

How our "ten" system works   32

Rubbish things about calculators   37

The long and short of it   45

Time?   52

Clocks   60

The quest for the right angle   72

The hard boys of maths   81

The magic square   103

Short-cuts   107

A really good magic trick   116

How to handle big numbers   125

Symmetry and the mindmashing maze   136

MURDEROUS MATHS
ARE YOU KIDDING?

City: Chicago, Illinois, U.S.A.
Place: Luigi's Diner, Upper Main Street
Date: 1 April, 1927
Time: 1:30 a.m.

Benni was leaning by the juke box waiting to mop the floor. All the tables had been cleared hours ago; all, that is, except one. The occupants were not men to be hurried unless you wanted to leave in a long wooden box. Benni watched the cigar smoke twisting up into the fan. He waited.

"Gentlemen, a toast," announced Blade Boccelli raising his glass. "As of this evening, the war between the east side and west side is now over. Let us drink to lasting peace between our families."

Benni watched amazed as the Boccellis and the Gabriannis solemnly clinked each other's glasses and shook hands.

"Luigi!" rasped One Finger Jimmy. "Wakey wakey! Time to go home!"

Benni watched as his sweating boss scurried over to the table and almost apologetically presented the bill.

"Twenty-three dollars and thirty-five cents," read the Weasel.

7

"So I guess we just split fifty-fifty, eh?" said Jimmy.

"Well you guess wrong," snapped the Weasel. "You guys all had the prawn salad, and that's ten cents more than fettucini."

"So? Your cousin there ate half my garlic bread!" snarled Jimmy.

"Half?" sneered Half-smile Gabrianni. "I ate one little piece. Besides, you offered it, you cheap scum."

"You calling me cheap?" In a flash Jimmy had pulled out his berretta. "How's about I offer you a couple of lead slugs?"

"Hold it guys," pleaded Blade, "we are friends, remember? We can sort this out. Who knows some maths?"

"I know we don't split fifty-fifty," said Weasel. "We pay less."

"But there's four of you and three of us," snarled Jimmy.

"You count pretty good for a guy with one finger," said Chainsaw Charlie. "Besides, your brother's so fat, he counts for two people."

"That does it!" said Jimmy leaping to his feet and upending the table. "He don't like being called fat, do you, Porky?"

"Sure don't," grunted Porky as he grabbed a long carving knife.

"Not so fast!" said the Weasel, pulling a machine gun from under his hat.

Benni and Luigi dived down behind the counter from where they could hear the sounds of shots, screams and bodies hitting the floor.

"Gee, it breaks my heart!" whispered Luigi. "If only they had got to know some maths."

"Yeah, and now they all gonna die," replied Benni.

"Who cares about that?" said Luigi. "I wanna know who's gonna pay the bill!"

9

Yes ... whether you're arguing over a restaurant bill, sending a rocket to the moon or you simply want to play a few tricks on your friends, you need to know a bit of MURDEROUS MATHS!

Some maths looks horrible, like this:

$$\int(x^3 + y^3)^{1/2}/\omega r = 0.27993$$

But that's just for weird boffins to worry about. Don't let it bother you!

Most of the best things in maths use very simple numbers, and some don't use numbers or letters at all! How about this:

A maths experiment to get you into hot water
- Fill a bath right to the very top.
- Get into it very gently.
- Lie down very gradually so that you are just about floating.
- Guess what? The amount of water that has just sploshed on to the floor weighs the same as you do!

When you get into trouble, just tell people that you are testing Archimedes' Principle of Hydrostatics, and he was one of the greatest mathematicians ever!

The first chapter starts with some easy stuff –
actually it's *so* easy that you could do it backwards
blindfolded upside-down while cutting your toenails.
Don't take it for granted, though, because even the
easiest maths can be murderous. In the first chapter
you will see how the whole human race could be
wiped out!

Impossible, you say? Well read on...

THE BASICS

Signs and symbols

You probably know what different numbers mean, don't you? 1 means *one*, 2 means *two* and so on, it's dead obvious.

As well as numbers, there are different signs you can use to show what you want these numbers to do.

= EQUALS

This is when two numbers are equal to each other, such as $3 = 3$. (Wouldn't it be great if all sums were as easy as that?)

+ PLUS

This is when you add two numbers together.

The thing to watch with "+" is that you must add up things that are the same. Look at this:

$$2 \text{ apples} + 3 \text{ apples} = 5 \text{ apples.}$$

(Some people might want to check this on their calculator. If you know a person like this then *run away* because they have got *brain rot.*)

Now look at this sum:

$$17 \text{ girls} + 9 \text{ boys} = 26 \ldots \text{whats?}$$

Is it 26 girls? No, unless your boys don't mind being called girls too. Is it 26 boys? No, unless your girls don't mind being called boys, but remember there are 17 of them and they could get pretty *tough.*

In fact it's 26 girls *and* boys, or even 26 children. Just because you counted them all together doesn't mean that some of them have to change from one to the other!

– MINUS

This sign is when you want to take one thing from another. Again, you have to make sure that both things are the same. This is all right:

$$7 \text{ dogs} - 4 \text{ dogs} = 3 \text{ dogs}$$

(Again, watch out for anybody who has to check this on their calculator. These are the sort of people who suck socks for a thrill.)

But what about this:

$$7 \text{ sausages} - 2 \text{ chips} = ?$$

You see! It's utterly daft and doesn't make sense.

× TIMES or MULTIPLY BY

Multiplying something is like adding something over and over again. 5×3 is like adding up three lots of five, *or* adding up five lots of three.

So $5 \times 3 = 5+5+5 = 3+3+3+3+3 = 15$

÷ DIVIDE BY

Dividing is the opposite of multiplying. It is like splitting a number up into equal pieces.

$$15 \div 3 = 5$$

This sum tells you that if you split 15 into three pieces, each piece is 5. Another way of saying it is "How many 3s in 15?" – the answer is still 5.

There is something rather cute about sums with dividing signs. You can swap the dividing number and the answer round and still be right.

Here you swap the 3 and the 5 over and get:

$$15 \div 5 = 3$$

It even works for big numbers like this:

$$12341 \div 43 = 287 \text{ is right, and so is}$$
$$12341 \div 287 = 43.$$

% PERCENT

This just means "divide by 100". Some schools give you results marked in percentages, so if you got 61%, that would mean you'd got 61 out of 100.

14

Shop windows quite often have notices saying things like "20% off". That would mean, "20/100 off", which is a way of saying that whatever they are advertising is $^1/_5$ of the price less than normal. Of course if you see a shop saying prices are "50% ON" then don't go in!

So, that's =, +, ×, ÷, and %. Cute, handy and fairly straightforward, but now for an explosive sign...

Powers

Quite often you have to multiply a number by itself a lot of times.

How about $13 \times 13 \times 13 \times 13 \times 13$?

Because the 13 here is multiplied by itself *five* times, this is called "13 to the *power* of 5". (Notice that this is *not* the same as 13×5, which is just 13 times 5.)

There is a short-cut to writing out these rows of numbers all the same. You just write a little number in the corner. So for $13 \times 13 \times 13 \times 13 \times 13$, instead of writing 13 out *five* times, you just put 13^5.

The exciting thing about *powers* is that you get some murderously massive numbers. Compare these two:

13 times 5 = 13 × 5 = 65

13 to the power of 5 = 13^5 = 371,293

How to scare a scientist

These numbers can be pretty scary, especially when it comes to things like *bacteria*! Bacteria look like very miniature alien maggots and they can live practically anywhere. (You've even got a few million friendly ones crawling round inside your guts!) There are thousands of different sorts, most of which are harmless. However, if you get enough of the dangerous ones, they can

be lethal! Scientists are always trying to invent new drugs to fight dangerous bacteria, but they have two. *big* problems...

● Although a drug might kill billions of bacteria, occasionally one or two become mutants. This means they can resist the drug and survive.

● Even if the mutant bacteria are lethal, one or two can't hurt anyone on their own. The trouble is that they can reproduce themselves rather quickly!

The bacteria guide to reproduction

1 Grow longer and split in half.

2 Both halves grow longer and split in half again.

3 Do this *every 10 minutes* (or even faster).

Indeed, if you start with just one lonely little bacterium:

- in 10 minutes you will have 2

- in 20 minutes you will have 2×2 (or 2^2)

- in 30 minutes you will have $2 \times 2 \times 2$ (or 2^3)
- in 60 minutes you will have $2 \times 2 \times 2 \times 2 \times 2 \times 2$ (or 2^6)
- in 24 hours you will have 2^{144} bacteria!

So how many bacteria will you have after just *one* day?

If you work out 2 to the power of 144 you'll find it comes to about: 22,300,000,000,000,000,000,000, 000,000,000,000,000,000,000! Murderous!

You can also write this number as 2.23×10^{43}. The chapter on Strange Numbers tells you all about this.

Actually, it's only the fastest types of bacteria that

can grow and split in 10 minutes or less. Most take around half an hour but even so, in one day you would get 2^{48} of them which is about 281,000,000,000,000. In two days you would get 281,000,000,000,000^2 which comes to about 79,200,000,000,000,000,000,000,000.

If this was a lethal bacteria...

- *and* there was nothing to stop it reproducing
- *and* it managed to spread itself
- *and* there was nothing to destroy it

... this would be enough to kill everybody in the world.

No wonder scientists are worried!

Isn't it amazing how fast numbers grow if you just keep doubling them? Watch out for Colonel Cancel who turns up later on in this book. Doubling numbers gives him a very nasty shock!

PROFESSOR FIENDISH'S FATAL FUNGUS

"Oh no, don't say I'm in perilous danger again!" you say with a yawn. But yes, it's the same old story ... Professor Fiendish has trapped you in his bathroom. On the floor is a huge patch of fatal fungus which is about to fire its *rot spores* all over the room. The only way to save yourself is to cover up the patch of fungus, not even a tiny bit must be left uncovered.

All you have to cover the fungus with is a set of *square* tiles which are all exactly the same size. (The edge of the pattern does not have to be neat just so long as you cover the fungus completely.) Luckily you find that this is easy...

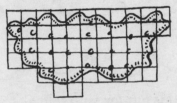

...but unluckily Professor Fiendish realizes it is *too easy* with square tiles! He takes them away and shows you some shapes like this:

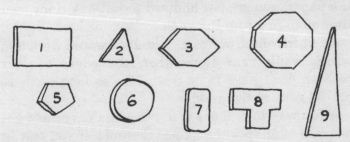

You have to choose just one of these shapes, and he will give you a set of tiles of that shape. Does it matter which shape you choose to cover the fungus with, or do you think that some shapes will not work?

Here's a clue: the round tiles would be useless because there would be lots of gaps between them like this...

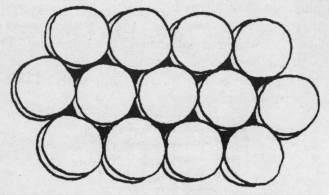

You can find this out for yourself. Get a lot of round coins such as 1p pieces and try to cover a piece of paper completely so that there is no paper at all showing underneath. (All the coins must be flat on the paper; you are not allowed to put any coins over the top to cover up the gaps.)

So which of the professor's shapes would work and which would not? Remember, the edges of your pattern don't have to be neat, just as long as there are no gaps in the middle.

A fun way to find out is to get some paper and cut out lots of shapes the same, then see if you can fit them together. That way you can see which shapes will save you from the fiendish fungus!

You could even invent your own shapes and cut them out. You should find that *any* shapes with three or four straight sides will work, but if you're clever you might like to see if you can invent shapes with five or more sides that work too.

The stirring saga of the valiant vectors

"Good grief!" exclaimed Colonel Cancel as he stuck his head round the guardroom door. "What is going on here?"

"Well you see, sir," stuttered the Sergeant, "it's like this. We've lost all our clothes."

The Colonel stared round in disbelief as his twelve Valiant Vector Warriors sat shivering in front of him.

21

"What do you mean you've lost your clothes?" gasped the Colonel. "I can see them from here all piled up in the corner. You should get your eyes tested."

"No, sir, we were playing cards and we lost them," mumbled the Sergeant trying to cover himself up with a pair of sevens and the jack of clubs.

"So who won them?" demanded the Colonel.

"How do you do?" said a small man stepping out from behind the pile. "Thag the Mathemagician at your service."

"Give my men their clothes back at once," demanded the Colonel.

"That wouldn't be proper," said Thag. "After all I won them fair and square, and these gentlemen, being gentlemen, wouldn't dream of taking back what wasn't theirs."

Around the room the Valiant Vector Warriors all nodded gravely. They knew that one of the main points of being a Valiant Vector Warrior was to be a gentleman, even though some of them weren't sure if being a shivering naked gentleman was such a good thing.

"Well, Mr Thag the Mathemagician, let's see how much of a gentleman you are," said the Colonel dealing the cards out, "because I'm about to teach you a lesson."

About ten minutes later...

"Can't I just keep my pants?" pleaded the Colonel. "After all I need somewhere to pin my medals."

Thag grinned. "You'll have to buy the clothes back," he said.

"How much?" asked the Colonel.

"You'll have to pay for each set of clothes separately," said Thag.

"How much?" asked the Colonel again.

"The first payment will be one pound. The second payment will be two pounds. The third will be three pounds. The fourth will be four pounds and so on."

"But there's thirteen sets of clothes including mine!" gasped the Colonel. "The last lot will cost thirteen pounds!"

"If you think that's too much, I'll give you a choice. The first payment could be one penny," said Thag.

"That's more like it!" said the Colonel.

"But the payments will double every time, so the second payment will be tuppence, and the next four pence and the next eight pence and so on."

"Piffle!" said the Colonel. "I'll go for the pennies.

Let me have my clothes back."

"I need a penny for the first lot," said Thag.

"Certainly," said the Colonel feeling for his pockets and only finding his belly button. "Oh … can I pay you later?"

"All right," said Thag, "but don't forget that for thirteen sets of clothes you'll need thirteen payments."

"You have my word," said the Colonel. "Besides, it's only a few pennies."

Soon all the soldiers were getting dressed again.

"Right!" said the Colonel turning to Thag. "What do I owe you?"

"No rush," said Thag, "who knows, there might be a few other little jobs I can do for you."

THUD! Just then an arrow shot through the window of the guardroom and slammed into the table right in front of Colonel Cancel.

"Good grief!" gasped the Colonel, "that was close."

"It was," agreed the Sergeant, "it nearly knocked the milk jug over."

"I'm going to have to complain about that postman," said the Colonel, as he untied a small roll of parchment from the arrow.

"What does it say?" said the Sergeant.

"Please read primes elephant help you I like cold sausages," muttered the Colonel.

"Eh?" said all the Vector Warriors together.

"It doesn't make sense at all," said the Colonel.

"Apart from the bit about cold sausages," said the Sergeant. "I like them too."

PLEASE READ PRIMES ELEPHANT HELP
YOU I LIKE COLD SAUSAGES AM NOT
IMPRISONED LOVE THOSE CURTAINS
IN GREEN CALCULUS DON'T WAIT UP
CASTLE HELLO MUM WATCH THE BIRDIE
SIGNED SEALED PRINCESS LONG JOHNS
UP-YOUR-JUMPER LAPLACE CRUMBLE
P.S. EGGS RHOMBIC BINGO WINDOW X

"Look," said the Colonel, "it says Princess."

"Princess Long Johns Up-Your-Jumper Laplace?" the Sergeant exclaimed. "Who's that?"

"Maybe it's Princess Laplace!" said the Colonel, "and she's writing in code."

"Code, by jingo!" gasped the Sergeant.

"Yes," muttered the Colonel, "and knowing the Princess it's bound to be one of those dashed fiddly number tricks."

"Oh gosh, sir, isn't she clever?" simpered the Sergeant. "Nobody will ever be able to decode her secret message."

"Including us," said the Colonel. "Brilliant. How are we ever going to know what she wants?"

A gentle cough came from the corner.

"I could decode it for you," grinned the Mathemagician.

"Really?" said the Colonel.

"But it will cost you one more payment!"

To be continued...

THE BEST INVENTION EVER

How do you feel about numbers?

The trouble is that numbers are so brilliant that everybody takes them for granted. In fact, *numbers are the cleverest and most powerful invention ever.*

You might think that telly is a much better invention, or a jet rocket is more powerful, but without using numbers to organize and calculate everything, they might never have been invented.

Handling numbers
or, Thank goodness we're not Roman!

These days we take reading and writing numbers for granted thanks to the system of using the ten numerical digits.

With our system you can write down a sum like this:

28
107
+ 654
= 789

In case you think that's a bit hard, look how the ancient Romans would have written out the same sum:

XXVIII
CVII
+ DCLIV
= DCCLXXXIX

Ugly, isn't it? The trouble was that in ancient times they didn't have our number system. The very earliest number systems worked like this...

People eventually realized that writing down lots and lots of little lines was a real nuisance, and they started to invent easier ways of doing it.

The Romans used lines for the smallest numbers, but as numbers got bigger they used letters as short cuts...

- Instead of drawing five little lines to show "5" they used the letter "V". They added more lines to the "V" if they needed to, so for example to show "7" they would draw "VII".

- To show the number "10" they used the letter "X". Again they would add more lines if necessary, so "13" would look like "XIII" and "15" would be "XV".

Eventually they ended up with this lot:

I = 1 V = 5 X = 10 L = 50 C = 100 D = 500 M = 1000.

CLEVERUS DICKUS

They say he invented the Roman number system

By combining these signs, they could show any number, e.g. 537 would be DXXXVII. So far so good! *But…*

They didn't always add the signs together. For instance, to write the number 9, they could have written VIIII, (which means 5 + 4), but it was easier to write IX. By putting the I in front of the X, that means you had to *take* 1 away from 10 to give the number 9. Murderous, isn't it? They used to do this with the bigger numbers too. XC was the same as LXXXX which is 90. XCII would mean 92, and XCIV would mean 94.

(Be honest, you're starting to think our system *is* pretty clever now, aren't you?)

Test yourself, can you match up the Roman numbers to ours? Be careful, because there are two numbers which don't match. Can you find them before your brain gets too hot?

DXXXIX XVIII LMV
DIX MMXXII CDIV
XLI MCMXCVII

955 539 404 2022 17 41 1997 1202

Answer: DIX and 1202 don't match.

Incidentally, there is one number that the Romans could NOT write down. Can you work out which one it is?

Even if you think that the Roman system wasn't so bad for writing numbers down, can you imagine having to do sums with it?

A Roman sum:

$$(MMCDLXIV \div XVI) + (XXIX \times XVII) = DCXXXXVII$$

Urghh!

31

How Our "Ten" System Works and the Invention of Nothing

If we want to write a number less than ten, we just put one digit down on its own, say 3 or 8.

Is it me, or is this a bit simple?

It's you, you're simple

If we want to write a number more than ten, we use more than one digit together. We can write the number "sixty-five" like this: 65. Or we can write the number "four hundred and eighty-two" like this: 482. We can even write *huge* numbers easily such as 98,746,227,021. (Imagine doing that in Roman numerals!)

Our system works because we can use the same set of digits, but they have different values depending on where you put them.

Take the number 531. We know that the 1 is worth 1, the 3 is worth 3×10 which is 30 and the 5 is worth $5 \times 10 \times 10$ which is 500. Each position is worth *ten times* more than the one on its right.

Suppose you used exactly the same digits but put them in different places, you would get a completely different number.

For instance, if you wrote them as 135, the 5 would now be worth just 5, the 3 is again worth

3×10 which is 30 (it's in the same place as before) and the 1 is worth $1 \times 10 \times 10$ which is 100!

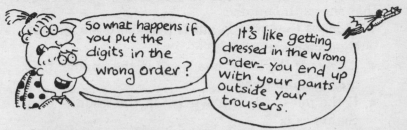

So what happens if you put the digits in the wrong order?

It's like getting dressed in the wrong order – you end up with your pants outside your trousers.

A number machine

In the olden days people had several different methods of recording numbers. They might use piles of stones or put knots in ropes, but the cleverest method was the abacus, and even today lots of people from Far Eastern countries still use them.

An abacus has rows of wires with beads on them. One sort of abacus has each wire divided into two sections with one bead on the top and four on the bottom. There is a bit of free room for the beads to slide along. Here is a small abacus...

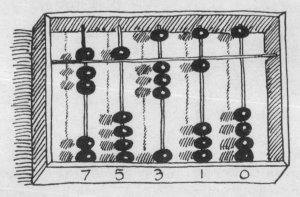

The position of the beads on each wire of the abacus shows a number.

When the single bead on a wire is pushed to the top, and the group of four is pushed to the bottom, that shows the number 0.

- If *one* of the lower beads is pushed to the middle, that means number 1.
- If *three* of the lower beads are in the middle, that means number 3.
- If the *top* bead on a wire is in the middle, that counts as 5.
- If the top bead *and* some bottom beads of the same wire are in the middle ... well, you can work it out!

The good thing about an abacus is that you can change the numbers very quickly without writing down and rubbing out. This means the abacus is helpful for doing adding and subtracting ... and in fact skilled people can even do multiplying and dividing faster than a calculator!

You can read off a number from the abacus, just like reading written digits. The abacus on page 33 shows the number 75,310. Just like written numbers, each wire on the abacus is worth ten times more than the wire on its right.

Have you noticed how everything seems to depend on the number *ten*? Does it seem odd, then, that we have *different* signs for all the numbers up to nine, but when we get to ten we *don't* have a special sign, we instead write a "1" followed by a "0"? These days we take it for granted, but in fact one of the major breakthroughs in the whole history of the world was...

The invention of nothing!

Even after the digits 1–9 had been developed, it took hundreds of years for people to realize they needed a sign for zero. It was easy on an abacus, you just left all the beads at the edge to mean zero. But when they wanted to write down the number two thousand and fourteen, they wrote 2 14. They just left a gap in the hundreds column ... if they remembered! As you can imagine, it could get very confusing:

Even though "0" is worth nothing, it means a lot! Can you imagine writing out large numbers if you didn't have any zeros? Now that *would* be murderous.

RUBBISH THINGS ABOUT CALCULATORS

... And how to keep Urgum the Axeman happy

These days calculators are everywhere. You can get them in watches, or on the side of pens. Gosh, soon there'll be raspberry-flavoured ones that you work with your tonsils. The trouble is that everybody has got very useless. Try asking somebody, "If I have six calculators and somebody pinches two of them, how many will I have left?" The chances are they'll say, "Ooh I dunno, where's my calculator?" However, calculators cannot do everything, and in fact sometimes they are complete *rubbish*.

The cake, the clot and the calculator

Picture the scene: suppose it's your birthday and you've got a cake you want to share with six friends.

You want to work out how much cake each person gets. What you are doing is some *maths* because you are dividing *one* cake by *seven* people (don't forget to include yourself!). Immediately one of your friends will turn out to be a complete clot and he will pull out a calculator and put in $1 \div 7$. He will then say that each person should get 0.142857143 of the cake. Can you imagine going up to a cake and trying to cut a piece which is 0.142857143 big? Of course not.

There are two things to do here. The first is to lock the clot in a cupboard and make smells through the keyhole. The second thing is to be jolly sensible and realize that you can now divide the cake by SIX which gives you a bigger slice. Of course, if you used a calculator to see what 1 divided by 6 comes to, it would give you an answer of 0.1666666 which again is a fat lot of good.

A much more sensible way of sorting the problem out is to realize that if six people are sharing a cake fairly, they will get one *sixth* of the cake each. (If you want to write a sixth down in numbers you just put ¹/₆). All you have to do to find out what a *sixth* looks like is to cut the cake into six equal pieces and hey presto, each one will be a sixth of the cake! It's like magic because without doing any hard sums in your head, you will automatically have multiplied the cake by 0.1666666 to make each piece. By gum, aren't you clever?

The calculator's problem is that it is no good at showing fractions.

Fraction facts

Fractions are numbers that are not nice *round numbers*. Round numbers are exact such as 1 or 2 or maybe 57 or even 193,679,032. If you ask how many people are in your school, you always get a round number such as 421, because you can't have half a person at your school. Of course some of them might be half-witted but that's different.

Fractions come in when the amount you're talking about is just a little bit more than one round number, but a little less than the next one. For instance seven and a half is bigger than seven, but not quite as big as eight.

Most sensible people write a half like this: $\frac{1}{2}$. But calculators can't do that because they can't write numbers underneath each other with a line between them. What calculators have to do is divide the 2 into the 1 and show the answer, which comes out as 0.5. At least that one is nice and simple and means exactly the same, but there are some fractions that even the biggest, poshest calculators cannot get exactly right. In fact...

Even the poshest calculators can be rubbish

Let's say you're dividing the cake by six again. How many digits can your calculator show at once?

Some can only show eight digits, and they will tell you that: $\frac{1}{6} = 0.1666666$

However, a posh calculator with a longer screen might be able to show twelve digits, and it will say that: $\frac{1}{6} = 0.16666666666$

So, which one is right? Well actually *neither* of them is exactly right. In fact if your calculator had a very long screen, and could show twenty digits, it would say: $\frac{1}{6} =$

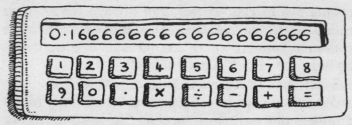

... and it still wouldn't be quite right!

Just out of interest, there are *two reasons* for not buying a calculator with a screen that can show a million digits.

1 It would not fit in your pocket (unless you were wearing some very funny shaped trousers).

2 It *still* wouldn't be absolutely right!

The trouble is that when you divide 6 into 1.0 (which is what the calculator is doing) you keep getting a teeny bit left over, and you have to keep dividing 6 into the teeny bit and you get an even teenier bit left over and so on.

Fraction patterns

Actually some fractions make pretty patterns on calculators. Go and unlock the clot from his cupboard, borrow his calculator and try these:

$1 \div 3 \quad 1 \div 9 \quad 1 \div 11$

One particularly interesting one is $1 \div 7$. If you had a very long calculator you'd find the answer came out something like:

0.142857142857142857142857142857...

Funny how numbers 142857 keep coming round again, isn't it?

That's why sometimes it's easier to work fractions out in your head and not bother with calculators.

There's *one final* reason calculators are no good at fractions. If you divide a calculator into halves, it won't work any more.

Five things to do with a dead calculator

1 Wrap it in silver paper and pretend it's a bar of chocolate.

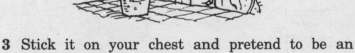

2 Hollow it out and use it as a very thin ice cube tray.

3 Stick it on your chest and pretend to be an android.

NO-IT-IS-NOT-PAST-MY-BED-TIME-I-AM-AN-ANDROID-WE-DON'T-HAVE-BED-TIMES.

4 Glue an aerial to it and tell everybody you've got a mobile phone.

Hello... Really? You want me to play for Chelsea?

41

5 Rent out the battery compartment for ants to live in.

oooh!
looks very
spacious

The thing about avoiding silly numbers like 0.16666 and 0.142857143 is that it keeps your head nice and clear, and you'll need a clear head if ever you come across...

Urgum the Axeman!
Urgum has three sons called Roy, Rod and Ron, but he doesn't have a daughter called Ruth. In fact they are all *ruthless*.

This is a photo of the daughter I never had .... sniff-

Urgum also has *eleven* axes. He has promised that Roy can have half of them, Rod can have a quarter of them and Ron can have a sixth of them. How would you help them share the axes out? ... and remember, these guys won't be happy if you get it wrong!

(The clot who was locked in the cupboard would probably get his calculator out and start by working out what a sixth of 11 is and then he would go and tell Ron he was going to get 1.8333 axes. Ron would then wonder what to do with the extra bit of axe, and then decide to use the clot for chopping practice.)

The answer is quite tricky, but just in case it ever happens to you, here's what to do...

First you will need to ask Urgum if you can borrow one more axe. Urgum will smile sweetly at you and say, "Sure, but make sure you bring it back or else ... har, har, har!"

Put it with the other axes to make twelve axes altogether.

Now then, Roy gets half of them which means you multiply the twelve axes by a half, which looks like this: $12 \times \frac{1}{2}$. This is the same as dividing 12 by 2, and the answer is 6. Roy gets *six* axes ... but before Roy takes them away, work out the others.

Rod gets a quarter of the axes (a quarter means the same as a fourth), so divide 12 by 4 and you'll see Rod gets *three* axes.

Ron gets a sixth of the axes, so divide 12 by 6 and you'll see Ron gets *two* axes.

"OK lads, help yourselves," you say.
Roy takes *six*, Rod takes *three* and Ron takes *two*.

Good grief! There's one axe left over. Hurriedly
you give it back to Urgum and run off as fast as you
can.

Can you see how this puzzle works? If you add up
the fractions each of the three boys has, this gives
you $\frac{1}{2} + \frac{1}{4} + \frac{1}{6}$ ... which does not quite make 1. (It
makes $\frac{11}{12}$.) When you borrow the extra axe, that
means you have twelve axes which makes the sums
easier, but because you only need to hand out eleven
axes, that means you have one left over to give back.

THE LONG AND SHORT OF IT

Do you know what long means? Is it different from short? Well believe it or not, the answer is *no*. Think about this old joke...

A man goes to the doctor, and the doctor says:

Are you laughing? Good, now keep laughing for four minutes. Go on, keep laughing for *four* minutes ... it's a long time four minutes, isn't it?

Or is it?

The man in the joke didn't think four minutes was a long time at all. The fact is that the same amount of time can be described as long or short, depending on what's happening.

Maybe you think *one second* is a short time, but in one second light can travel 187,000 miles. If you were daft enough to hold a red hot coin in your hand for one second, it would seem like ages.

If you think a hundred years is a long time, go and find a talking rock and ask it how old it is. In fact, if you find a talking rock in less than one hundred years, then you've been very quick.

Time isn't the only thing that's confusing when it comes to length. A motorway one metre long would be very short, but if your nose was a metre long, then it would be very long. In other words, your nose would be stupidly long and the motorway would be stupidly short even though they were the same length! Incidentally, if your nose *is* one metre long, and you happen to be standing next to a motorway one metre long, be careful or you might get a traffic cone on your conk. Anyway, here's the ultimate "long" joke...

You don't have to laugh for four minutes at this joke, but it's so funny you probably will do anyway.

The mystery continues...

"Well?" asked Thag the Mathemagician. "Do you want me to decode the Princess's message or not?"

"Very well, and you will have your fourteenth payment," agreed Colonel Cancel. "So what does it mean?"

"The clue comes in the first three words – 'Please read primes'," explained Thag the Mathemagician. "You know what prime numbers are, don't you?"

"Well, men? Who's volunteering to tell him?" said the Colonel, pretending that he knew himself.

The Vector Warriors all looked sheepish. They preferred volunteering for things like having to make the tea when they were supposed to be on marching practice.

"A prime number is a number that cannot be divided exactly by any other number except itself and one," said Thag.

"Of course," said the Vector Warriors in unison.

"They haven't a clue what I'm talking about, have they?" asked the Mathemagician.

"Erm, well divisions aren't as a rule part of the normal military procedure," explained the Colonel.

"Can they arrange piles of bricks?" asked the Mathemagician.

"I should say so," said the Colonel. "It's one of their favourite pastimes."

"Give each man a different number of bricks, and tell them to arrange the bricks neatly in rows. They must not leave any gaps or have any bricks left over."

"Will this help crack the code?" asked the Colonel.

"Eventually," said Thag. "Meanwhile I'm going to number the words in the message."

| 1 | 2 | 3 | 4 | 5 |

PLEASE READ PRIMES ELEPHANT HELP
YOU I LIKE COLD SAUSAGES AM NOT
IMPRISONED LOVE THOSE CURTAINS IN
GREEN CALCULUS DON'T WAIT UP
CASTLE HELLO MUM WATCH THE BIRDIE
SIGNED SEALED PRINCESS LONG JOHNS
UP-YOUR-JUMPER LAPLACE CRUMBLE
P.S. EGGS RHOMBIC BINGO WINDOW

"Now then," said Thag, "to understand this message, we only read the words which have prime numbers."

"So what's dividing got to do with it?" asked the Colonel. Thag took him over to where one of the warriors had been arranging his bricks.

"This chap here has ten bricks," explained Thag. "He has arranged them in two neat rows of five. This means you can divide ten neatly into two lots of five. Ten isn't a prime number."

"Oh!" said the Colonel catching on, "so we don't read the word 'sausages' then?"

48

"No, we can cross it out," said Thag.

"Pity," said the Sergeant, "because I like sausages, you know..." but Thag and the Colonel had moved on.

"Now this chap here has thirteen bricks," said Thag.

"And he's made them into three neat rows of four bricks," said the Colonel.

"Ah yes, but he has one brick left over, so thirteen doesn't divide neatly."

"Suppose he makes three rows of five bricks?"

"He'll find he's two bricks short. There's no way you can break thirteen bricks up into smaller rows."

"So thirteen is a prime number!" said the Colonel, hoping he was right.

"Yes it is, so 'imprisoned' is one of the words we have to read."

"Good grief!" said the Colonel. "Which other numbers are prime?"

"Numbers two, three, five, seven…" started Thag.

"Nine?" asked the Colonel.

"No, because you can put nine bricks into three rows of three. Eleven is the next prime number and then thirteen."

"So reading those prime numbers, the message starts, 'Read primes, help I am imprisoned…' Great Scott!" gasped the Colonel. "It's an emergency!"

He turned to his valiant troops. "Great news chaps! We've been invited to an emergency. It's probably going to be perilously dangerous and trouser-wettingly scary. Your chances of survival are bound to be tiny and there will be little or no reward."

Somehow the troops did not seem to share his enthusiasm.

"Not even any sausages?" asked the Sergeant.

"No. Sadly we've had to cross sausages out," admitted the Colonel. "But just think of the excitement!"

The warriors thought about it and decided that staying at home and playing with neat little rows of bricks was just about the right amount of excitement for them.

50

"Hmm," said Thag, "do you know where Calculus Castle is?"

"Of course," said the Colonel.

"Well, according to this message, Princess Laplace is imprisoned there in a room with a rhombic window," said Thag.

"A rhombic window?" said the Colonel. "But how will we know which one that is?"

Thag grinned at him. "It'll cost you another payment," he said.

To be continued...

TIME?

How time got started...

Silly as it may seem, everything to do with time is based on the sun coming up and going down. Every time the sun comes up and goes down, we call it a day, and the amount of time between summers we call a year.

Giving days different names

As soon as days and years were invented, some clever person invented the *personal organizer*. Ancient personal organizers don't look much like the modern ones, but they lasted a lot longer. If you go to Egypt, you can see ancient personal organizers carved out on great big bits of rock. They weren't very handy for slipping into your inside pocket, but at least the batteries never went flat and nobody could pinch them. Can you imagine ancient people walking round with their personal organizers?

"I say Hippopotty, can you do lunch next year?"

"Let me just check my big bit of rock. When do you want it?"

"On a day."

"But they're *all* called day!"

This was useless of course, which is why people thought of more detailed ways of dividing the year up.

The ancient Romans had a system which is pretty close to what we all use now. First of all they divided the year into months and even now some of our months are still called after Roman Emperors. August is called after Augustus and July after Julius Caesar. (Mind you, maybe Caesar wouldn't be very pleased because they made his name sound a bit like "Julie".)

If I wasn't dead I'd invade you again!

The Romans then gave names to some of the days of the month, and one of the most famous early dates was "the ides of March". Ides was the Roman name for the fifteenth day in the month and one morning Caesar was strolling around Rome when out jumped a chap who shouted, "Beware the ides of March."

Caesar thought it was just another nutter, but sure enough on the 15th of March, Caesar was stabbed to death by all his government ministers. It came as a bit of a surprise to him as he had thought they were all his best chums, but then that's government ministers for you.

Giving numbers to days in the month started to

catch on, and soon every day in the year had its own date such as "the twenty-fourth of July" or "the second of October". This made having a party easier because if you said what date it was on, it meant that everybody would turn up on the same day.

Splitting up the day

Halfway between sunrise and sunset, the sun is as high in the sky as it is going to get. The moment when this happens has lots of names, such as "midday", "noon" and "about lunchtime", but the technical name is "the meridian". People decided to split the day into two halves called "before meridian" and "after meridian", but irritatingly for us they did it in *Latin*. The Latin word for "before" is "ante" and the Latin word for "after" is "post" so the day was split into "ante meridian" and "post meridian", which gets shortened to a.m. and p.m.

So far then, you can plan things in your personal organizer to the nearest half day. This is fine when your life is nice and simple. Suppose you are a sheep, you could plan your organizer like this...

No problems there. However, imagine phoning the station and asking when the next train to Glumthorpe is leaving. "In the afternoon," isn't much help. Either you'll have to sit there for hours waiting, or you'll chance going a bit later and probably miss it. Unless you're a sheep (or a station announcer), time needs to be more accurate.

To start with, the day was divided into 24 hours and these were numbered in two lots of twelve. That meant there were 12 hours in the morning (from midnight to midday) and 12 hours in the afternoon (from midday to midnight). This helped all sorts of people such as monks who wanted to plan their church services through the day, and sailors who wanted to know when they were supposed to be on watch or in bed.

Twenty-four might seem like an odd number to choose, but at least it divides up nice and neatly into halves, quarters, thirds or sixths. Twenty-three hours a day would have been a real pain. Imagine what a clock face would look like!

Hours are nice comfortable lumps of time but unfortunately people got fussy and started to say things like...

when am I getting a tea break?

What time is the kick-off?

When is the next train to Glumthorpe?

So each hour got split up into sixty minutes. Sixty is another good number because it splits nice and neatly into all sorts of bits such as halves, thirds, quarters, fifths, sixths, tenths...

Of course, people then went one better and split each minute up into sixty seconds, and luckily for most of us, that's the smallest bit of time we need to worry about.

How to cope with time

Even though there are years, months, days, hours, minutes and seconds, you don't need to use all of them at once. Suppose it's your birthday and you send out an invitation like this:

One of two things will happen...

1 Everybody will arrive at 28 minutes and 12 seconds past 7 and get jammed in your doorway.

2 They will think you're a bit strange and decide not to come at all.

Of course, the seconds are far too short to worry about so leave them out. A few minutes don't matter so much, so just say "half past seven" or 7:30. On the other hand a year is so long, it's usually obvious which one you're talking about so you don't really need to put that in either.

When you miss these extra details out, it gives you room on your invitation to put much more important things:

IT'S MY BIRTHDAY

Please come to my party

on

15th May 1999

at 7·30pm

and

Don't forget to bring me a big present

There are some events whose exact time does tend to be given in more detail than others. Astronomers are probably the worst people for getting silly about this. They sit at their computers and charts for days and then proudly tell you that there will be a complete eclipse of the Sun at 19 seconds past 8 minutes past 4 o'clock on the morning of 5 January in the year 2167. Funnily enough the same people can also be very vague about other times, such as:

CLOCKS

Clocks measure time and help you answer one of two questions...

1 What time is it?

2 How long did something take to happen?

When you are asking, "What time is it?" you are actually asking about *absolute time*! That sounds posh, doesn't it? With absolute time you will get an answer like "ten minutes past three".

When you are asking how long something takes, such as, "How long does Uncle Tommy spend in the bathroom?", then that's *relative time*! You will get an answer like "twenty-three minutes and eleven seconds". Relative time doesn't tell you *when* Uncle Tom has his bath, you just find out how long it takes.

Absolute time

Here's one of the best facts to know about absolute time...

The only clock that can't show the wrong time is a sundial. As the sun moves across the sky, a pointer in the middle of the sundial casts a shadow showing what time it is. (Of course, if the sun isn't shining it won't show anything, but at least it won't be showing the *wrong* time.)

You might say this is rubbish, but think about it. Suppose you have a watch and it has stopped, how do you know what time to set it to? There's a choice of things you can do:

1 Look at the time on another watch or clock.
2 Turn on the telly and see if there's a clock showing. If you've got teletext you can see the time on that.
3 Phone up the speaking clock (which is a stupidly expensive way to find out).
4 Go outside and find a sundial and wait for the sun to come out and look at it.

Of course methods 1, 2 and 3 are all quite accurate and will give you the time to the nearest minute or even second. A normal small sundial can only give you the time to within about 15 minutes.

However ... suppose *all* the electricity in the world suddenly stopped *and* every wind-up clock and battery clock went wrong, which is the only method left of telling the time? Yes, it's the good old sundial! It might not be accurate to fractions of a second, but it will always be working for the next few million years!

The reason a sundial is special is that all other clocks can only show how much time has passed since they were set. Even the most expensive clock in the world has to be told what time it is when it is started up. From that point onwards, all it is doing is counting off the seconds and telling you how far it has got!

Old types of clock

Very old clocks didn't bother with minutes, they just showed roughly which hour it was. There were several different types...

Wind-up clock There are still some of these cranky old monsters about and they are wonderful. One of the first was built 600 years ago and was powered by a weight that weighed nearly a quarter of a tonne! They didn't have minute hands and in fact some didn't even have an hour hand, they just rang a bell every hour!

Candle clock People used to have special long candles with marks down the side. As the candle burnt down, it would reach the marks one by one and so indicate how much time had passed. Candle clocks were often used through the night in churches to tell monks when the late services should start.

Rope clock This is an ancient Chinese version of the candle clock where they would light one end of a knotted rope and let it slowly burn along.

Hourglass The sand slowly trickles through from the top of a glass container to the bottom. Like the candle clocks, you have to know what time you started it going, and then guess how much more time has passed by the amount of sand that has fallen through.

Water clock (or clepsydra) These clocks are a cleverer version of hourglasses, but they use water instead of sand. They could have all sorts of extra pipes and clever gear systems fitted to help show the time.

How accurate are clocks?

The earliest clocks used to be pretty awful at keeping the right time, but about 400 years ago the pendulum was invented which would swing backwards and forwards at an exact speed and so keep the clock more regular.

Balance wheels on springs came in, and these were particularly useful for watches. If you get a chance to look inside a wind-up watch, you'll see a hollow wheel with a curly spring inside it going backwards and forwards. This is doing the same job as a pendulum does for a big clock.

These days nearly everybody has a "quartz" watch or clock. Quartz is a sort of crystal, and with the battery connected it sends out very regular electric pulses. The clock just counts the pulses and converts them into seconds going past. (The quartz crystal is working like a pendulum but 100,000 times faster!)

The most accurate clocks are atomic clocks. They are similar to your quartz clock, but instead of using a quartz crystal, they count the vibrations of special atoms. Atomic clocks are so accurate, they are even more accurate than the earth going round! Using these clocks, scientists have worked out that some days the earth takes up to five thousandths of a second more to spin round than others. (You can't help wondering if scientists really have nothing better to do sometimes, can you?)

64

How does a clock show you the time?

There are two main sorts of clock display...

- the old-fashioned clock face and hands
- the "digital" clock which just shows you a row of numbers.

It doesn't matter which sort of clock you've got, they should both tell you the same time.

Clocks don't usually bother telling you whether it's the morning or the afternoon, because it's so obvious. For instance, if a clock says half past two, and the sky is black, you can be pretty sure it's half past two in the morning.

The most important thing on an old-fashioned clock face is the hour hand (which is usually the smallest). The hour hand moves right round all the numbers on the clock face twice in a complete day. If a clock only has an hour hand, you can only tell which hour of the day you've reached.

Clock with just an hour hand shows it's the hour between one and two o'clock. Not much use.

Clock with hour and minute hand shows it's about 28 minutes past one. More useful.

Clock with second hand too shows it's 14 seconds before 28 minutes past one. Even more useful.

Clock with lots and lots of hands. Absolutely no use at all.

When you have a minute hand as well, you can tell which minute of the hour you've got to. With a second hand, you can be really accurate because you'll know how long you've got until the next minute. If a clock has a second hand, you can always tell which one it is because you can see it moving. (The other hands are moving too, but far too slowly for you to notice.)

If you think that the second hand is the most useful because it is the most accurate, look at this:

A clock with just a second hand. Absolutely useless for telling the time.

Although a clock with just a second hand is useless for showing *absolute time*, it is the most helpful when you want to measure *relative* time. Suppose you wanted to see how long it took to run up and down the stairs, the second hand would show you exactly how many seconds it took. You couldn't do that with a sundial!

The numbers on a digital clock work in just the same way as the hands on a face clock.

9:54:53

HOURS : MINUTES PAST : SECONDS PAST
               HOUR   MINUTE

If there are two numbers, then it's like a clock with just an hour and a minute hand. If there are three numbers then the last number is how many seconds have passed.

There are two little complications to watch out for with digital clocks.

1. If there are more than thirty minutes past the hour, you can describe the time in two different ways. In the clock at the bottom of page 66, you could say the time is "nine fifty-four". However it's neater to say "six minutes to ten".

2. Often a digital clock has a "twenty-four-hour" display. (Railway station clocks always have a twenty-four-hour display.) A twenty-four-hour display just lets you know if it's morning or afternoon. Don't panic if you see a time such as 17:21. If the hours number is bigger than twelve, then you have reached the afternoon. You just subtract twelve from the hours number and find out what time it is. A clock that says 17:21 is just telling you that it is twenty-one minutes past five in the afternoon.

Sheerluck Homes and the Duchess's diamonds
or, Time to tell the time

"My diamonds!" wailed the Duchess, "they were in this little box on my dressing table, but now they've gone!"

"Hmmm!" said Sheerluck Homes, the ace detective as he looked around the room. "It seems the thief was in a bit of a hurry and knocked your clock on to the floor."

"Who could be so heartless as to break a little clock?" sobbed the Duchess. "What use is it now?"

"A lot of use, actually," said Sheerluck. "The hands on the clock have not moved since it hit the floor, so they show the exact time the crime was committed."

"I want to speak to all the people who had the opportunity to sneak into your room this afternoon," said Sheerluck.

"But that could be anybody in the house!" gasped the Duchess. "Oh no! They would have seen my unmentionables drying on the radiator."

Sheerluck glanced round to see a massive expanse of frilly pink lace quietly steaming away in the corner. The Duchess was right, they were indeed unmentionable.

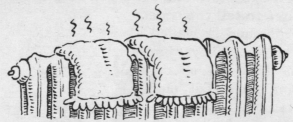

Later, in the library, the household staff and guests were assembled and a uniformed police officer guarded the door.

"I need to check what each of you were doing this afternoon," said Sheerluck.

"I was on the lawn making daisy chains with Millicent," simpered Primrose Poppett, "and we heard the cuckoo clock chime five ever so sweetly."

"That clock's always fifteen minutes fast," muttered Colonel Grunt.

"And where were you, Colonel?" asked Sheerluck.

"In the shed, polishing my blunderbuss," came the reply. "I caught the cloth in the trigger and the damn thing went off, bang. According to my twenty-four hour digital watch, that was at 14:46 hours precisely. Somebody must have heard it."

"So that was you, was it?" sniggered Rodney Bounder. "Silly old fool."

"And precisely where were you, sir?" asked Sheerluck.

"Oh ho! You can't pin it on me!" sneered Rodney. "I was playing cards with the vicar. You can ask him."

"What time was that?" asked Sheerluck.

"When I looked at my gold and diamond watch, it was about a quarter to five," sneered Rodney. "Anyway, stop wasting everybody's time. I say the butler did it."

"Hear hear," grunted the Colonel.

"It was my afternoon off," whispered Croak the butler, "I took my sister Aggie to the station and put her on the 4:46 train."

"Well one of you sneaked into the Duchess's room during the afternoon and did a despicable deed," said Sheerluck. "And not only that, you probably caught sight of the Duchess's green undies on the radiator."

"Green? But they were pink!" came a voice.

"Hah!" exclaimed Sheerluck triumphantly. "I thought it had to be you! Constable, arrest that thief!"

Can you tell who gave the mistimed alibi?

How to test your calculator

Do this sum:

$12345679 \times 9 =$ (don't forget to miss the 8 out)

See what answer you get! *One* will find it obvious if *one's* calculator is a good *one*!

THE QUEST FOR THE RIGHT ANGLE

... And how not to shoot yourself with a cannon

"No no no!" screamed the Abbot. "Those books will not do!"

"What's the matter?" said the Monk.

"Look, the corners are all the wrong angles!"

"What's an angle?" asked the Monk.

"It's a way of saying how big corners are," said the Abbot. "And those corners are either too big or too small. These books won't fit into neat piles, they'll fall off shelves, and the pages will open all over the place. Look, here's how a book should be, all the corners are exactly the same."

"In fact all the corners are the *right angles!*"

A lot of other angles

This rather silly story explains what a right angle is. Right angles are nice square corners. If a corner is murderously sharp then it's an acute angle, and if it's not sharp enough, it's an obtuse angle. There's even a word for an inside-out angle: a reflex angle.

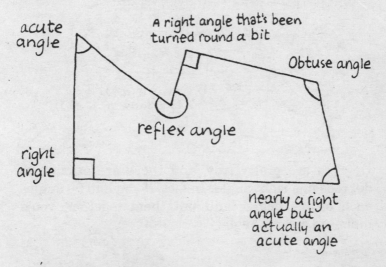

acute angle

A right angle that's been turned round a bit

Obtuse angle

reflex angle

right angle

nearly a right angle but actually an acute angle

It's easy to remember which is the *acute* angle. Imagine a very, very, very acute angle ... like the point of a pin. It would be pretty sharp, eh? Well, some people are described as acute if they're pretty sharp. (Not sharp as in you could cut your finger on them, but sharp as in having nifty brains and so on.)

There's something really stupid about angles and that is they are measured in "degrees". The problem with calling them degrees, is that the weather-forecaster uses degrees to say how hot it is. Maybe this all started because the first person to start measuring angles was called Mr Degree and he wanted to be famous. Anyway it would have been much better if angles were measured in "bendies" or "twiddles". You could even make your own word up, it's bound to be less confusing than saying degrees. It also stops maths teachers making really pathetic jokes like...

Degrees are pretty tiny, and there are exactly 90 degrees in a right angle. In fact, if you had 90 angles each of one degree and put them together, you'd make up a right angle.

Some very tiny angles

90 one degree angles put together

Adding angles
Now then, look what happens when you put two right angles together:

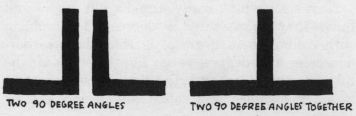

TWO 90 DEGREE ANGLES   TWO 90 DEGREE ANGLES TOGETHER

You get a straight line! In fact, if you want to be all clever, you could tell people that a straight line is actually an angle of 180°. ("Degrees" gets a bit boring to spell out all the time, so people usually write ° instead.)

Oddly enough this number 180° is rather interesting. Triangles have three corners, and the angles of the corners always add up to 180°. This is something you can prove *without doing any boring old sums*! All you need is a bit of paper and some scissors.

1 Cut a triangle out of the paper. Any shape of triangle will do but remember the sides have to be straight.

2 Tear the three corners off your triangle.

3 Put them together like this:

4 Jump up and down with glee shouting, "Look! There's a straight line along the bottom and a straight line is 180°, so the three angles together make up 180°."

(By the way, are you still waiting to see how not to shoot yourself with a cannon? Well, you'll find out in a minute, but in the meantime don't go firing any cannons.)

So anyway, now you know about triangles having 180° in them. What about squares? Look at this book. It's fairly squarish, but the main thing to note is that is has four corners and four sides. (Flat things always have the same number of corners as sides.) If a shape has four straight sides, the angles add up to *two* lots of 180° which is 360°. What does this mean, eh? Well, do what you did for triangles ... cut out a shape with four straight sides. (If you like you can just cut out a triangle then chop one of the corners off.) Tear off the corners and put them together, and see what happens! You should get something like this:

They all fit together without leaving a gap in the middle! It even works if you cut out a shape with a reflex angle.

Actually it doesn't matter how many corners a shape has, you can easily find out how many degrees the angles add up to. Just divide the shape up into triangles by drawing lines between the corners. (Don't draw any lines that cross over.)

Look at the shape with seven corners. You'll see that it's been divided into triangles in two different ways, but each time there are five triangles. Because there are 180° in a triangle, in this case the five triangles have $5 \times 180°$ in total (which makes 900°), and that's what the angles in a seven-cornered shape add up to. Of course if you can't be bothered with dividing things up into triangles, then just count the corners, subtract two and multiply by 180°, and that's the answer.

The cannon question

All right, all right, so what's this got to do with cannons? Well, when you fire your cannon, one of the things you have to set is the *elevation* of the barrel, which is a posh way of saying how far up in the air it will be pointing. The elevation is measured in degrees. An elevation of zero degrees means the cannon is pointing straight along the ground. Here are some elevations:

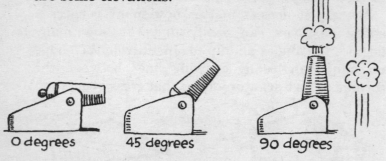

O degrees   45 degrees   90 degrees

Can you see which one should *never* be used? Yes, the 90° elevation will just shoot the cannon ball up in the air and it will land *biff* on your head. Although 90° is called a right angle, with cannons the right angle is definitely the *wrong* angle.

So what's all the fuss about?

A classic old trick

- Write down any three-digit number. The digits have to be different.

I've written down...

671

- Write it down again with the digits the other way round.

That turns into 176

- Subtract the smaller number from the larger one.

Easy! 671-176=495

- Write this answer down backwards.

That makes 594

- Add the two new numbers together.

SO, 495 + 594 =

- Your answer is 1089!

1089

GASP! HOWDUDOODAT?

If you want to try this trick on your friends, write "1089" on a piece of paper and put it face down on the table before you start. Whatever three digit number they choose to start with, they will be amazed when you show them the answer!

WARNING: Just occasionally the answer will be 198. In this case, tell the person to write the answer backwards again (891) then add the two together, and get 1089!

THE HARD BOYS OF MATHS

How can you tell mathematicians from real people? Here is a guide...

● They dribble when they read the telephone book.

● They usually have one trouser leg accidentally stuck in the top of their sock.

● They look like they are wearing wigs, even when it's their real hair.

● They never understand good jokes, but laugh uproariously at weird things like furniture, road maps and shampoo bottles.

● They have bits of yesterday's dinner stuck on their chin.

● They stare at the telly when it isn't on.

And most telling of all...

● They wear brown suede shoes with black laces.

Yes, one or more of these signs is usually a dead give-away, but this was not always the case. In fact, over the last 5,000 years mathematicians have included some of the coolest people in history!

Druid priests

Ancient people were easily intimidated by anyone showing a bit of brain. In particular the changing seasons and phases of the moon were very important to them, and so if you could predict when winter was coming or, better still, when there might be an eclipse, you had it made.

Nearly 5,000 years ago strange structures like Stonehenge were built, and one theory says they were to help the mathematicians of the time calculate this sort of thing. It's hardly surprising that they used to be regarded as magicians with extraordinary powers. They may even have made sacrifices to the sun and moon, which goes to prove ... mathematicians could get away with murder!

Thales

In ancient Greece maths was as popular as pop music or sport is to us today. There was a lot of hot competition to prove and develop basic theories and around 550 BC Thales, an olive-oil tycoon, became a big star by laying down some of the absolute fundamentals. Does this mean he was a bit on the boring side? Not really … to celebrate one of his discoveries, he went out and *sacrificed a bull to the gods*! The poor bull lost out after Thales found that any angle in a semicircle (see picture) is always a right angle.

Pythagoras
Pythagoras carried on from Thales and founded a religious mathematical cult who worshipped numbers. There were lots of rules for his disciples, one of which was never to eat beans!

OLYMPIC NEWS

STILL ONLY ONE GOLD COIN

PYTHAGORAS CALLS FOR TOTAL BEANS BAN SEE PAGE 2

PHEW WHAT A STINKER!

IT WAS REVEALED TODAY THAT A RANDOM BEANS TEST ON OLYMPIC CHAMPION FARTACLES HAS PROVED POSITIVE HE LATER ADMITTED EATING EIGHT PLATEFULS TO HELP HIM BREAK THE WORLD POLE VAULT RECORD WITHOUT A POLE.

WOW

WHAT A PONG

FARTACLES YESTERDAY

Pythagoras did lots of clever stuff including how harmonies in music work, but his biggest hit was proving that...

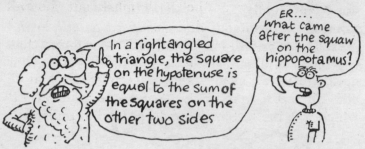

It's easier to understand what he means by looking at a picture.

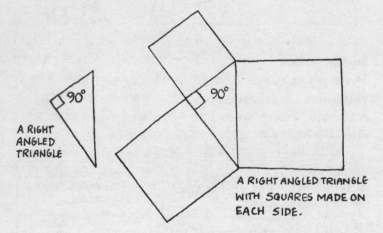

A RIGHT ANGLED TRIANGLE

A RIGHT ANGLED TRIANGLE WITH SQUARES MADE ON EACH SIDE.

A right-angled triangle is any triangle with a right angle (at 90°), and the "hypotenuse" is the longest side, which is always opposite the right angle.

If each side of the triangle is made into a square, all Pythagoras is saying is that the total size of the two smaller squares is exactly the same as the big one. Sounds a bit dull, eh? Don't you believe it, this rule has helped people build bridges and skyscrapers. It even helps to mark out football pitches!

Pythagoras and his followers were so madly in love with numbers that they went a bit potty. They decided that all even numbers were female and all odd numbers were male except the number "1" which was the father and mother of all numbers...

...but when it was found that some problems could not be solved with their nice neat numbers, it drove them so mad that they tried to pretend it wasn't true...

Maths wars

Hard to believe, isn't it? But yes, people did argue and even fight over who had the best theories and proofs.

Because Pythagoras and his gang were so clever, there were others like the Eleatics who couldn't resist annoying them by finding murderous problems that their methods could not solve. The hero of the Eleatics was Zeno who loved inventing paradoxes. These are things that *look* true but *can't* be!

Zeno's paradox of the runner and the tortoise

A runner can move ten times as fast as a tortoise. However, if the tortoise starts one mile away, the runner will never catch him! Think about it...

ONE MILE

The runner runs one mile ... but in the meantime the tortoise has moved one tenth of a mile, so the tortoise is still one tenth of a mile in front of the runner.

ONE TENTH OF A MILE

The runner then runs the extra tenth of a mile ... but the tortoise has moved on just a little bit more.

ONE HARDLY ANYTHINGTH OF A MILE

The runner runs the next little bit, but while he does so, the tortoise moves on just a tiny bit more ... and so on! Even though the gap between them might be teeny weeny, *the runner will never quite catch the tortoise*.

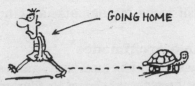

GOING HOME

Of course, we know that the runner can catch the tortoise, but it's very hard to prove!

Euclid

The great thing about brainy people arguing is that it makes them think harder and so they come up with increasingly clever stuff. Around 300 BC another Greek called Euclid collected all the best proofs and theories that the old maths gangs had come up with and put them in his book, *Elements*, which has become one of the most famous books in the world.

Euclid himself was a bit of a Pythagoras fan and came up with some theories of his own, including a rather natty proof that prime numbers are unlimited. *Elements* contained just about everything worth knowing about basic maths, and it inspired the next lot of mega mathematicians including...

The awesome Archimedes

Archimedes is one of the all-time greats. To realize how brilliant he was, you have to remember that all he used was a pencil, a ruler and a compass. At the time there wasn't even a decent system of writing numbers down and doing calculations! Here are just some of the things he invented...

Giant lever systems
These were so powerful that his home town, Syracuse in Sicily, used them to grab and smash enemy ships! Archimedes realized that lever power was so strong that he once claimed, "Give me a place to stand on and I can move the earth."

The Archimedean Screw
This is like a coiled pipe which when revolved seems to make water flow uphill!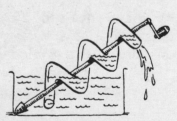

The Sand Reckoner A mega number system. In his time there wasn't a good way of writing massive numbers so he invented one. It was based on the myriad which is 10,000. He called a myriad of myriads (which is 100 million) "the first order of numbers". He then multiplied a myriad of myriads by itself a myriad myriad times (this is getting to be a *very* big number) and then multiplied that by itself a myriad myriad times. If you wanted to write the answer out you would have to write down a 1 followed by *eighty thousand billion zeros*! Archimedes said this number was "quite adequate".

.. a myriad myriads and one, a myriad myriads and two...

Honest! There's a bloke over there counting sand

NAAAAAH!

..DOING-..

GERONIMO!

Mirror

lens

enemy

Giant catapults These were also used by the Syracuse army to smash invading forces.

A solar ray gun! Legend has it that he devised a set of mirrors that could focus the sun's rays onto enemy boats and set them on fire!

Brainstorm in a ... bath!
Despite all this brilliance, Archimedes is probably

best known for jumping out of his bath and running down the road stark naked shouting, "Eureka!"

In fact "Eureka" means "I have found it!", but what had he found? Remember right at the beginning of the book you filled your bath up and got into it – well that's what this is all about...

The King had suspected that his new crown was not solid gold, and had asked Archimedes to try and find out. In his bath, Archimedes realized that when you put an object into a full bowl of water, the amount of water that spills over tells you exactly how big the object is. He weighed the crown, but when he put it in water he found the crown was bigger than it should have been if it had been made of pure gold. This was because cheaper, lighter silver had been used instead of some of the gold. This was good news for Archimedes, but very *bad* news for the cheating goldsmith!

Since he had that bath, Archimedes went on to discover a lot more about how and why things float or sink. If he'd skipped his bath and had a shower instead, we might have never known how to design ocean liners and submarines.

WORK WORK WORK

The triumph of the sphere

Archimedes's personal favourite invention wasn't his deadly catapults or his clever engineering machines, it was this murderous little equation:

$$Vs = 4\pi r^3/3$$

This equation tells you how to calculate the exact volume of a sphere. A sphere is a round shape like a ball. The little "r" in the equation is the radius of the sphere, which is the distance from the very middle to the edge. The funny little "π" sign is called pi, and it equals roughly $3^1/_7$.

What Archimedes did was prove that a sphere is exactly two-thirds as big as the smallest cylinder it will fit inside. Or in other words, if you had a solid ball which would only just fit inside a tin can with the lid on, the ball takes up exactly ²/₃ of the space inside the can.

He was so proud of this discovery that he had a little sign of a sphere in a cylinder put on his gravestone.

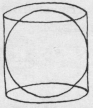

Even with all his monstrous war machines defending the town, the Romans managed to invade one night while everybody was having a *wild* party. Lots of town people were murdered, but the Roman general Marcellus had especially ordered that the 75-year-old Archimedes should be spared. Unfortunately a soldier found him doodling in the sand and Archimedes upset him by saying, "Do not disturb my diagrams," so the soldier killed him.

A gruesome end to the Greeks!
Although Archimedes lived in Sicily and was educated in Egypt, he was actually a Greek. After he died, the Romans took over the Greek empire and maths stopped being so trendy. Some people liked it, but they didn't get much encouragement. One of the last was a very clever woman called Hypatia who used to attract huge audiences at her lectures around AD 400.

Sadly the Christians thought she was a pagan and decided her fans needed discouraging. One day she was pulled off her chariot and dragged to the church where "her flesh was scraped from her bones with sharp oyster shells and her quivering limbs were delivered to the flames."

You never realized that being a maths teacher could be so dangerous, did you?

The maths mafia

One of the last ancient Greek mathematicians was Diophantus, and he has been nicknamed "The Father of Algebra". Algebra is a special way of presenting maths puzzles which have one or more mystery numbers for you to work out. The mystery numbers are shown by letters (the letter x is especially popular). Some of these are dead simple, and others, murderous.

Here are some algebraic equations with their different names. *Don't panic!* You don't have to solve them unless you really want to.

Mm mmmmmm mm mmmm mmmm mmmm m mmmmm *

* NO THANKS I'D RATHER CHEW A SLUG

- Very simple algebra equation: $x = 6 + 2$
  This is a LINEAR equation. Can you see that x equals eight? Dead easy!

- A bit harder: $2x^2 + 3x = 27$
  The x^2 means this is a QUADRATIC equation.

- A *lot* harder: $5x^3 + 7x^2 + 2x = -16$
  The x^3 means this one is CUBIC.

- Mercy! $3x^4 - 5x^3 + 9x^2 + 2x = 43$
  The x^4 means this one is QUARTIC.

- Total brain destruction: $3x^5 + 41x^4 - 2x3 - x^2 + 7x = 3$
  The x^5 means this is called, "ARGH, I think I'm going to be sick!"

AAAARGH!

94

More than a thousand years after Diophantus died, algebra started to really take off in Italy. Some pretty nasty characters including cut-throats and card cheats developed a great interest in solving harder and harder algebra puzzles. They liked to show off how clever they were by having competitions, and they often bet a lot of money on who they thought could solve them – just like in a boxing match today.

OK champ - let him lead off with the linear equation then hit him with the quadratic - cubic combination

One match was between a man called Fior and another nicknamed "Tartaglia", which means "Stammerer". (Hardly surprising really: when he was a boy someone had shoved a sword through the top of his mouth!) They handed each other some very tough sums to do, and eventually Tartaglia won. Not only did he pick up the money, he had also discovered a method of solving a whole range of tough algebra equations. (The *cubic* equations.)

Soon after this he was approached by Girolama Cardano who must have been a really shady character. Among other things he was an astrologer, a doctor, an author, a gambler, a friend of the Pope and the father of a murderer. Cardano smooth-talked Tartaglia into giving away his secret method, and immediately ran off and published it in a book. This same book included a way of solving the even harder quartic equations invented by Lodovico Ferrari.

At last ... a wimpish mathematician?
So far then, everybody involved in maths seems to have been pretty tough or got up to dubious deeds or both. However, we've just come across Lodovico Ferrari ... the man who cracked quartic equations.

The amount of brain power needed just to understand quartic equations is massive, and solving them is twice as hard. Therefore you might think that Lodovico Ferrari was a timid little chap with a weedy moustache who always went shopping with his auntie.

Wrong! Lodovico used to drink, gamble, swear and fight, and in the end he was poisoned to death by his own sister.

Lodovico's last words

I thought that *!3⊘*3⊖ pasta tasted funny

Other oddballs
There are umpteen other odd people who were famous mathematicians. Have you heard of the

book *Alice in Wonderland*? It's brilliant and funny, but a bit weird! It was written by a man calling himself Lewis Carroll, but by now you won't be surprised to know that his real name was Charles Dodgson and he was a mathematician from Oxford. He used to specialize in logic and died about 100 years ago. (Maybe you've heard of The Mad Hatter's Tea Party, or Tweedledum and Tweedledee or even the Queen of Hearts who played croquet with flamingoes and kept shouting, "Off with her head!". Lewis Carroll was the one who made them all up!)

How about the French teenager Évariste Galois? Just before he died at the age of twenty he scribbled down some algebra theories he'd thought of and years later people realized he was a maths superstar. However, he used to fail exams, fight teachers and was locked up for threatening the King. He died in 1832 in a duel over a woman ... a murdered mathematician.

The list of dubious characters in maths goes on and on (like the American Professor who does all his thinking while riding about on underground trains!), but to name them all would make this book very strange, so let's hurry on to something else.

The rescue continues

Meanwhile, at Calculus Castle terrible things were happening. High in a tower the Princess Laplace was imprisoned and being forced to count to *infinity*. It wasn't going well...

"...three hundred and thirty-nine million, four hundred and twenty-eight thousand, nine hundred and fifty-nine. Three hundred and thirty-nine million, four hundred and twenty-eight thousand, nine hundred and sixty. Three hundred and thirty-nine million, four hundred and twenty-eight thousand, nine hundred and sixty-one..."

Poor Princess, she had hardly started. Down on the ground the Valiant Vector Warriors were looking round blankly.

"We can hear her voice," said the Sergeant, "but we don't know where it's coming from."

"The message suggested the rhombic window," said the Colonel.

"Which one's that?" said the Sergeant. "They are all different shapes."

They all turned to look at Thag. "Are you sure you can afford a fifteenth payment?" he said.

"Of course, it's only pennies, man!" said the Colonel.

"Fair enough," said Thag. "A rhombus is a shape with four sides of equal length."

The warriors all turned back to examine the windows.

"You mean a square," said the Colonel seeing a large square window at the bottom of the tower. "That's got four sides of equal length."

"Yes, a square is a sort of rhombus," admitted Thag, but before he could continue, the Colonel had turned to his men.

"This is it men!" he shouted. "Rescue party – *charge!*"

"*Taran-tarrah,*" cried all the Valiant Vector Warriors and they hurled themselves at the big square window.

"*Ouch!*" was the next thing they all cried as they were blasted by a concentrated stream of differential calculus, which is the deadliest maths ever invented.

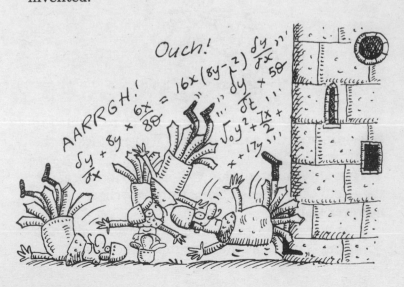

99

"The fiend!" muttered the Colonel. "Baron Calculus has booby trapped the rhombic window."

"Don't worry," said Thag. "A square is only one sort of rhombus. Most rhombuses look rather different." So saying he picked up four sticks and lashed them together to make a square.

"If all the sides are the same length, then it has to be a square," muttered the Colonel.

"No it doesn't," said Thag as he pushed two opposite corners of his model together. "What does this look like?"

"A diamond!" said the Colonel. "You're right, the sides are still the same length! We've attacked the wrong window!"

"Hurrah!" shouted the Vector Warriors because they felt they needed something to cheer about, however feeble.

"I can see the diamond window," said the Sergeant, "but it's at the very top of the tower."

100

"Go and borrow a long ladder," said the Colonel.

"How long do you want it?" asked the Sergeant.

"Just for the afternoon," said the Colonel.

"No," said the Sergeant, feeling confused, "I mean how long in length?"

"I dunno," said the Colonel. "We need to know how high the tower is but all we have is a tape measure."

"I'll hold the bottom of the tape, you walk up the wall and take the other end to the top," shouted one of the warriors. Ribald laughter followed because Vector Warriors have a really sad sense of humour.

"I know how you can measure the tower," said Thag the Mathemagician, "but..."

"I know, I know, it'll cost a sixteenth payment," said the Colonel.

"Are you *really* sure you can afford it?" asked Thag.

"Pah, it's only pennies!" said the Colonel. "Besides, are you sure you can walk up walls?"

"That won't be necessary," grinned Thag.

To be continued...

Beat the calculator

Get a friend with a calculator to put in any three digit number and tell you what it is. Then, as quickly as possible, he or she must...

● multiply the number by 7
● multiply the answer by 11
● multiply the answer by 13.

It doesn't matter *how fast* he or she tries to do it, you will be able to write the answer down first!

All you do is write down the original number twice! So if the original number is 838, you write down 838838 ... and that will be the answer!

THE MAGIC SQUARE

There are all sorts of good tricks you can play with numbers, and the magic square is one of the oldest. Here's a very simple magic square to start with:

8	1	6
3	5	7
4	9	2

The numbers 1–9 have been arranged so that you can add up any straight line of three numbers and you always get the same total – 15. It works for all three horizontal lines, all three vertical lines and both diagonals. Here's another even better magic square:

8	11	14	1
13	2	7	12
3	16	9	6
10	5	4	15

This square uses the numbers 1–16 and the magic number is 34. You can get 34 by...
- adding up any straight line of four numbers (horizontal, vertical or diagonal).
- adding the four corners.

- adding the four in the middle.
- splitting the square into four quarters, and adding the four numbers in any quarter! (e.g. the bottom left quarter would be $3 + 16 + 10 + 5 = 34$.)
- removing the four numbers in the middle *and* removing the four corners. Add up the numbers remaining on the two sides ($13 + 3 + 12 + 6$) or the numbers remaining on the top and bottom ($11 + 14 + 5 + 4$). What do you get?

This magic square is brilliant because you don't have to have 34 as your magic number. You can make your own magic square to come out with any number you like! Look at this square again.

8	11	14	1
13	2	7	12
3	16	9	6
10	5	4	15

There are four *key* numbers which are on black squares. If you want the magic number to be different from 34, you only have to alter these four key numbers!

Suppose you would like your magic number to be 25. Because 25 is 9 less than 34, all you do is write the square out again, but subtract 9 from each of the four key numbers:

8	11	5	1
4	2	7	12
3	7	9	6
10	5	4	6

There you are! Every line and combination of numbers as before will now add up to 25!

If you're making a birthday card, you could make up a magic square that adds up to the person's age! Maybe your granny is 103 years old, in that case you can work out that 103 is 69 *more* than 34, so add 69 to each of the four key numbers.

Here's a very special magic square!

96	11	89	68
88	69	91	16
61	86	18	99
19	98	66	81

All the usual combinations of four numbers come to 264. BUT ... turn it upside-down and see what happens!

And finally ... here is an even bigger magic square which uses all the numbers from 1–25. Every straight line adds up to 65. Check it!

17	24	1	8	15
23	5	7	14	16
4	6	13	20	22
10	12	19	21	3
11	18	25	2	9

SHORT-CUTS

Anybody who doesn't rely on calculators all the time always looks cool, so would you like to be one of them?

What you have to realize is that a lot of sums have short-cuts. So look at these and make maths less murderous for yourself!

Times 10

The *easiest* short-cut of all is when you need to multiply a whole number by 10. All you do is put a "0" on the end!

$$3,785 \times 10 = 37,850$$

If you want to multiply by 100, put "00" on the end.

$$4,558,566,385,465 \times 100 = 455,856,638,546,500$$

Multiplying by 1,000 or 10,000 or even 1,000,000,000 is as easy, just put the extra zeros on the end.

Adding a zero only works with whole numbers. If you have a decimal number like 6.247, you just move the decimal point along to the right. It's easy!

So $6.247 \times 10 = 62.47$ or $6.247 \times 100 = 624.7$

Times 99 or 9

Isn't it irritating that so many things in shops cost 99p? Suppose you want to buy thirteen books at 99p each, what does that come to?

First of all you need to realize that 99p is the same as 100p – 1p. This is easy! $13 \times 100p$ is just £13. From this subtract 13p and get the answer which is £12.87!

$13 \times 99 = (13 \times 100) - (13 \times 1) = 1300 - 13 = 1287$

Of course multiplying by 9 is very similar, it's just the same as 10 – 1. Suppose you need to do the sum: 67×9. It's just the same as $670 - 67$ which is easy to work out as 603.

Times 5 or 25

To multiply a number by 5, it is often easier to multiply by 10 then divide by 2.

$$377 \times 5 = 3770 \div 2 = 1885$$

To multiply by 25 is also easy! All you do here is multiply by 100, then divide by 4.

$$143 \times 25 = 14300 \div 4 = 3575$$

When will numbers divide?

Sometimes it's helpful to know when you can divide one number into another neatly without any remainder.

10

Ten is the easiest! Any number that ends in a 0 will divide by 10, all you do is knock the 0 off!

2

Two is also very easy. Any *even* number (i.e. any number that ends in 2, 4, 6, 8 or 0) will divide by 2.

5

Five is easy too. Any number that ends in a 0 or a 5 will divide by 5.

3

Three is really fun! Add up all the digits in the number. If the total divides by 3, then the number will divide by 3! Let's see if 7845 will divide by 3.

Add up the digits: $7 + 8 + 4 + 5 = 24$. Does 24 divide by 3?

Add up the digits: $2 + 4 = 6$...

Yes! So 7845 will divide by 3!

9

Nine works the same way as 3. Add up all the digits, if the total divides by 9 then the number will divide by 9!

Does 15673 divide by 9?

Add up the digits: $1 + 5 + 6 + 7 + 3 = 22$.

Oh dear! 22 does *not* divide by 9, so 15673 doesn't either!

6

As $6 = 3 \times 2$, you just need to do two simple checks. Does the number divide by 2? Does the number divide by 3? If the answers are both *yes*, then the number will divide by 6!

4

Just take the last two digits of your number. Will they divide by 2? If they will then do it. If you can divide the answer by 2 as well, then the whole number will divide by 4.

Does 23855632 divide by 4?

Take the 32 and divide by 2: $32 \div 2 = 16$

As 16 will divide by 2 as well, then 23855632 *will* divide by 4.

Basic instinct

One really useful skill you can develop is "getting the feel" of when an answer is right. This stops you making mistakes, especially with multiplying. It could even mean you don't end up accidentally paying too much in shops! Here are some hints to help you...

1 The answer can only be an odd number if *both* the other numbers are odd.

$3 \times 7 = 21$

2 If one number ends with a 5, the answer always ends with 5 or 0.

$13 \times 5 = 65, 22 \times 35 = 770$

Answers can only end in a 5 if one of the numbers does.

3 If one number ends with a 1, the answer ends with the same number as the other number.

$471 \times 28 = 13188$

(28 ends in an 8, so does the answer.)

4 Check the size of answers, make sure there aren't too many or too few digits! $23 \times 49 = 87$ ... the answer is obviously too small. How about $17 \times 6 = 9820$ ... the answer is too big!

Have a look at these sums ... but don't work them out! Just *guess* which of the answers is right. You'll be surprised how easy you find it with a bit of practice!

$37 \times 28 = 91$ or 1036 or 743

$100 \times 28 = 2880$ or 28000 or 2800

$99 \times 99 = 9801$ or 9999 or 999

$7 \times 13 = 178$ or 98 or 91

$21 \times 33 = 691$ or 692 or 693

You can check your answers on a calculator.

If you want to get really good, then challenge a friend. Make some sums up for each other like the ones above with a choice of answers. The one who gets the most right the fastest is the Champion Number Cruncher! The best part about it is, the more you do it the better you will get!

And finally, not a short-cut!

7

If you want to test if a number divides by 7, it is a bit more complicated, but it is rather a nice mystery!

- Write down your number, e.g. 3976
- Knock off the last digit: 397
- Multiply the rest by 3: $397 \times 3 = 1191$
- Add the last digit to the answer: $1191 + 6 = 1197$
- Does this divide by 7?

DO IT ALL AGAIN!

- $119 \times 3 = 357$
  Add the 7 = 364: Does this divide by 7?
- $36 \times 3 = 108$
  Add the 4 = 112: Does this divide by 7?
- $11 \times 3 = 33$
  Add the 2 = 35: Does this divide by 7?
- $3 \times 3 = 9$
  Add the 5 = 14: Does *this* divide by 7?
- $1 \times 3 = 3$
  Add the 4 = 7 YES!

So 3976 *does* divide by 7, but it's quicker just to go straight ahead and try it!

The saga goes on

"All right, you'll get your sixteenth payment, but how will you measure the height of the tower without walking up the wall?" asked Colonel Cancel.

"All I need is a straight stick," grinned Thag slyly, "and let's hope the sun doesn't go in."

The Valiant Vector Warriors looked on as Thag stuck the stick in the ground so it pointed straight up. Most of them were wondering what getting a suntan had got to do with measuring towers.

"Now we measure the height of the stick," said Thag.

"But the Princess isn't at the top of the stick," said one Vector Warrior. Everybody else sniggered, but if they were honest, they weren't sure why this was such a stupid remark.

"Now then," said Thag, "we wait until the shadow of the stick is as long as its height."

So they all waited as the sun set a bit and the stick's shadow got longer. In the background they could hear, "...three hundred and thirty-nine million, four hundred and twenty-eight thousand, nine hundred and eighty-four..."

"Now!" shouted Thag suddenly making everybody jump. "The shadow of the stick is exactly the same length as the height of the stick."

"Hurrah!" shouted the warriors, pretending to understand why this was such a good thing.

"Quick, measure the shadow of the tower," said Thag.

"The shadow is thirty metres long," came the result.

"Then thirty metres is the height of the tower," said Thag.

"How do you know?" gasped the Colonel.

"Easy," said Thag. "When the stick's shadow is the same length as the height of the stick, then the tower's shadow has to be the same length as the height of the tower."

"Why?" sneered the Sergeant suspiciously.

"Similar triangles," said Thag.

"Obviously," said the Colonel, who secretly wondered where the triangles were.

"Look at it another way," said Thag. "If the stick was one metre high and the shadow was the same length, it would be one metre long, right?"

"Right!" chorused all the warriors.

"If the stick was twice as high, the shadow would be twice as long, right?"

"Right!" chorused all the warriors again.

"And if the stick was thirty metres high, the shadow would be thirty metres long, right?"

"Right!" chorused the warriors happily. They liked simple choruses.

"But instead of a thirty-metre stick, here we've got a thirty-metre tower, right?"

"Right!" sang all the warriors except the Colonel. He was a bit worried as to how a thirty-metre stick had suddenly turned into a massive stone tower, but he decided to keep quiet.

Soon a ladder was leaning up against the tower wall.

"Right," said the Colonel. "Who wants the privilege of rescuing the Princess?"

The thirty-metre ladder looked very long and wobbly.

"Well lads?" he insisted. "Don't be shy."

"Actually, I've got a note from my mum," said one warrior.

"I'm allergic to rungs," said another.

"I've just washed my hair," said a third.

The Colonel was getting desperate.

"Now then chaps, you know I'd go myself if it wasn't for my bad knees," said the Colonel.

"Yeah, they've turned to jelly," came a voice.

"Seriously, I'll offer a fifty pound bonus to the man who goes up."

The warriors looked up at the ladder again. Fifty pounds was a lot of money but unfortunately thirty metres was a lot of ladder.

The Colonel turned to Thag. "How about you?" he asked.

"It'll cost you the seventeenth payment," said Thag.

"Is that all?" said the Colonel. "I was going to offer you fifty pounds!"

"I tell you what, I'll give you the choice," said Thag. "Would you rather give me the seventeenth payment or fifty pounds?"

"The seventeenth payment of course!" laughed the Colonel. "It's only pennies!"

Thag gritted his teeth and started up the ladder.

To be continued...

A REALLY GOOD MAGIC TRICK

Good grief! A magic trick in a maths book? Could it be...

- turning your teacher into a melon?

- making the sofa disappear?

- pulling £1,000 out of your nose?

No, it's better than that, it's the
AMAZING UPSIDE-DOWN CARDS TRICK!
This trick has got the two main requirements of any magic trick...

- It will baffle anybody who hasn't read this book.
- It is dead easy to do.

All you need is a pack of playing cards, a big cloth

such as a towel, a table and somebody to play the trick on. Here's what happens...

1   You shuffle the pack of cards. If you drop a few on the floor you can be all cool about it and don't bother picking them up. (This will fool people even more!) You put the pack face down on the table. If you trust your friend to follow your instructions properly without cheating, you can shut your eyes for the rest of the trick!

2   Tell your friend you have a magic number, which is *thirteen*. Ask your friend to count *thirteen* cards off the pack and turn them face-up.

3   Ask your friend to slot the face-up cards back into the pack one by one, so they are all separated. The pack will then be a mixture of face-down and face-up cards. Afterwards your friend can shuffle the pack (but make sure he or she doesn't turn any cards over when they do it).

4   Ask your friend to count thirteen cards off the top of the pack without turning any of them over. Ask him or her to put them down in a separate pile away from the others and cover them with the cloth. If you had your eyes closed you can open them now.

5   Tell your friend that *without looking*, you are going to turn over some of the cards under the cloth. You put your hands under the cloth and say some magic words. (Make sure these are pretend magic words. If you use real magic words your friend might turn into a jelly or something which would be a bit awkward.)

6   Remove the cloth, leaving the pile of thirteen cards.

7 Here's the magic bit! Get your friend to examine the two piles. Your friend will find that there is exactly the same number of face-up cards in each pile!

1. Shuffle

2. Count thirteen Cards face up

3. Slot cards back in pack & shuffle

4. Count thirteen Cards from top of pack

5. Turn cards under cloth

6. Take away cloth Hey presto!

The great mystery of this trick is that you hardly touched the cards, and didn't even have to look at them!

Your friend will wonder how you could possibly know how many turned-up cards were left in the main pile, and will wonder even more how you managed to get the same number in the small pile *without looking*!

So how did you do it? The answer is that when you

put your hands under the cloth, you just turn over the WHOLE pile of thirteen cards. That's all!

When you put your hands under the cloth, it's even more fun if you pretend you are doing something really complicated. If you pull a silly concentrating face as if you are feeling the cards, your friend will spend hours later on feeling the cards himself to see how you did it. Ha ha!

Your friend will already be desperately trying to work out how you did the trick, but now here's the *really* good bit. Put all the cards face down, shuffle the pack and do the whole trick again...

...*But* this time your friend can choose his or her own magic number. (Numbers between 9 and 15 are best but any number will work, although it gets boring if the number is much higher than 20.) Instead of thirteen, just use whatever number your friend wants and do the trick again.

How does it work?

This trick is easiest to explain with some simple algebra. If you haven't come across algebra before you might think URGH, but algebra is just a neat way of explaining things without lots of words and waving your arms about. (See page 93 for an explanation.)

Get a pack of cards and follow the trick through like this:

● Take 13 cards off the top, turn them face up, slot them back into the pack and shuffle.

- Take the top 13 cards off the pack, and look at them. You should see that some of the cards in your little pile are face up. Count them.
- Let's say there are 4 cards face up in your little pile. This means that in the main pack there must be 9 face-up cards left. (Because there were 13 face-up cards altogether and you've got 4 of them in your little pile. $13 - 4 = 9$.)
- Now, look at your little set of 13 cards again. If there are 4 facing up, all the rest must be facing down which means 9 cards are facing down.
- If you turn your little pile over … what do you get? Your 4 face-up cards will turn face down, and your 9 face-down cards will face up!

- So you will end up with 9 face-up cards in your little pile, which is the same number as the 9 face-up cards in the main pile!

First, let's see where the number 9 came from – it's because we keep taking 4 away from 13. In fact, instead of writing 9, we could write 13 minus 4 or $(13 - 4)$ all the time.

We put brackets round little sums such as $(13 - 4)$ to show we mean a number, otherwise people might think $13 - 4$ was a football score or the date of your birthday or something.

Let's see our instructions again…

- Take 13 cards off the top, turn them face up, slot them back into the pack and shuffle.
- Take the top 13 cards off the pack, and look at them. You should see that some of the cards in your little pile are face up. How many are there?
- Let's say there are 4 cards face up in your little pile. This means that in the main pack there must be $(13 - 4)$ face-up cards left.
- Now, look at your little set of 13 cards again. If there are 4 facing up, there are $(13 - 4)$ cards facing down.
- If you turn your little pile over ... what do you get? Your 4 face-up cards will turn face down, and $(13 - 4)$ cards will face up!
- So you will end up with $(13 - 4)$ face-up cards in your little pile, which is the same number as the $(13 - 4)$ face-up cards in the main pack!

Suppose that when you first looked at your pile of 13 cards you found there were 7 cards facing up? Or 2 cards? Or even 0 cards? It would be a real nuisance writing out the instructions above lots of times for each number, so *algebra* uses a sort of code...

Let the letter "F" equal the number of cards that

were face up in your little pile. (You could choose any letter you like, but "F" is easy to remember in this case because it means "Face up".)

Let's write out the instructions again but in *algebra*...

● Take 13 cards off the top, turn them face up, slot them back into the pack and shuffle.

● Take the top 13 cards off the pack, and look at them. You should see that some of the cards in your little pile are face-up. How many are there?

● Let's say there are F cards face-up in your little pile. This means that in the main pack there must be $(13 - F)$ face-up cards left.

● Now, look at your little set of 13 cards again. If there are F cards facing up, there are $(13 - F)$ cards facing down.

● If you turn your little pile over ... what do you get? Your F face-up cards will turn face down, and $(13 - F)$ cards will turn face-up!

● So you will end up with $(13 - F)$ face-up cards in your little pile, which is the same number as the $(13 - F)$ face-up cards in the main pack!

The great secret of algebra is that a letter always means the same number all the way through. So if you got 3 cards turned up to start with, just swap all the Fs in the instructions for 3s and you would see how that worked!

If you look at the last line of the instructions it tells you that there are $(13 - F)$ cards in the little pile and $(13 - F)$ cards in the main pack. $(13 - F)$ is always the same number, it doesn't matter how big or small F is. (Suppose when you first looked at your pile of 13 cards and didn't find *any* cards face up, F would equal 0. The sum still works!)

When we first described the magic trick, we said that the magic number did not have to be *thirteen*, in fact the trick works with any "magic" number. Algebra can describe this too!

Let's let the letter "M" stand for our magic number.

For the last time, let's see the instructions.

- Take M cards off the top, turn them face up, slot them back into the pack and shuffle.
- Take the top M cards off the pack, and look at them. You should see that some of the cards in your little pile are face-up. How many are there?
- Let's say there are F cards face up in your little pile. This means that in the main pack there must be (M − F) face-up cards left.
- Now, look at your little set of M cards again. If there are F cards facing up, there are (M − F) cards facing down.
- If you turn your little pile over ... what do you get? Your F face-up cards will turn face down, and (M − F) cards will turn face up!
- So you will end up with (M − F) face-up cards in your little pile, which is the same number as the (M − F) face-up cards in the main pack!

There you are! Algebra has proved this magic trick always works. Next time you play this murderous trick on somebody, if you feel really nice you can write out a complete explanation for them. Just copy out the instructions, but instead of using "M" put in whatever magic number they pick. Instead of using "F" put in how many cards were face-up in the pile you were given.

Hey! Get this, Erica knows a magic trick using someone called Algy's bra!

How to make a calculator friendly

Push these buttons on a calculator in *exactly* this order:

$2 \times 2 \times 2 \times 2 = \times 3 \times 3 \times 3 \times 3 = -2 - 3 - 2 = \times 2 \times 3 \div 100 \div 100 =$

Turn the calculator *upside-down* and look at the answer!

HOW TO HANDLE BIG NUMBERS

Have you ever heard something like this on the news...

Or you might be told that the moon is a quarter of a million miles away, or even that there are 800,000 different sorts of insects.

Does something strike you as a bit fishy? Yes ... isn't it odd how these things always seem to be an exact number! Why is that?

It's because when numbers get big, nobody can be bothered to be accurate. Imagine a newsreader announcing:

You'd forget what they were saying before they even finished, so what people tend to do is "round numbers off".

Rounding off numbers and how Gladys tried to save her love life

Suppose you've got 61 sweets, it's close enough to say you've got about 60, isn't it? All you've done is make the last 1 into a 0.

This is called *rounding down*. In general, if the last number is a 5 or more, then round it up to 10, but if it is 4 or less, round it down to 0.

Rounding off – the love story

It's amazing what people do when they're madly desperately and pathetically in *love,* isn't it? This is the story of Gladys – actually this person doesn't have to be called Gladys, it could be anybody such as your grumpy big brother or the silly woman you see in the post office ... but just for convenience here, it's Gladys.

Gladys is desperate because the most fanciable person in the whole universe is supposed to be coming round but *hasn't turned up.* As she tries to pretend that she's not bothered, she ends up doing the weirdest things. In fact she's just opened a tin of beans and counted every one. It came to 1,928. Poor Gladys.

Suddenly her smelly little brother comes in. "Counting beans," he sniggers, "because you've *bean* stood up? How many are there?"

Gladys doesn't want to admit to him that she

counted exactly, so she rounds the number off. "About 1,930," she says after rounding *up* the 8.

In comes Gladys's mum who is all bright and cheery.

"Counting beans, dear?" she says to Gladys. "That's nice. How many do you make it?"

Gladys is getting very embarrassed, so she rounds the number off even more to try and show she really doesn't care. "1,900," she mutters, "but that's only approximate."

Here she ignored the 8 completely, just looked at the 2, and rounded it *down.*

Suddenly the doorbell goes and in walks Dreamboat Fancy Pants who spots the beans immediately!

"Hello darling warling sweetie pudding pie!" gushes Gladys who has gone utterly purple and is laughing like a burst drain. She realizes that it's still far too embarrassing knowing

there's about 1,900 beans in a tin, so in her head she

calls it 2,000. (She ignored the 2 and the 8, and just rounded the 9 up to 10.)

"I hear you've been counting the beans in a tin," says Dreamboat Fancy Pants.

Arghh! Mega-cringe! Gladys just wants to *die*.

"So how many are there then?" Dreamboat asks.

"Quite a lot," she says with a slight yawn as she tries to be as utterly cool as possible.

This is not called rounding up or rounding down. This is called being desperate.

"Is that the best you can do?" says Fancy Pants. "When I did it I got 1,928."

There are two things to learn from this:
- You can round numbers off just a bit, or a lot depending on how accurate you want to be.
- Everybody does stupid things like counting baked beans sometimes.

SO: that's how Gladys's love life, rounding off and beans are all linked, and remember folks ... you read it here first.

Seriously big numbers!
Sometimes people try and tell you interesting things but you just can't remember them! Here's one...

The average distance to the Moon from Earth is 238,906 miles.

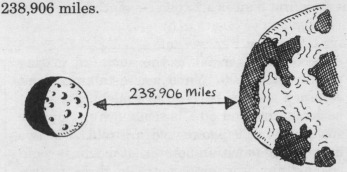

238,906 miles

See the problem? That number is easy enough to read from a book, but it's a pain if you wanted to remember it! To make it easier, we can round this number off. Here's some results of rounding the distance to the Moon...

239,000 miles   This is rounded to *three* digits. (Because after the first three digits we have put zeros.)
Accuracy rating: 99.8%

240,000   This is rounded to *two* digits. (Because here we only give the first two digits and then put zeros.)
Accuracy rating: 98%

200,000   This is rounded to *one* digit, but is very inaccurate and never used!
Accuracy rating: 80%

Usually we say the distance to the Moon is "a quarter of a million miles" because it's easy to remember. This is the same as 250,000 miles so it's still accurate enough for most purposes (accuracy rating 95%).

Generally things are rounded to two digits but if the very first digit is a 1 then it's much better to use three digits.

A percentage (or %) is the same as getting points out of 100. When you're talking about accuracy, 100% is perfect, 90% might just about be acceptable and 50% is really awful. Suppose you're buying a snake and are told it is two metres long to within 50% – that means it could be anything from one metre to three metres long! Useless eh?

OK, now you've got the hang of a mediumly big number, hold on to your pants because here we go!

Let's get into some *really* big numbers! What would *you* call a big number? Ten? A hundred? A thousand? How about a million? How about *a million million*?

Wouldn't it be good if you won a million million pounds? Even though this is quite a big number, you could still write it down in your savings book. It would look like this: £1,000,000,000,000. And you would look like this:

To make it clearer how big the number is, we put a comma between every three digits, but sometimes this is not enough...

Do you know how many atoms there are in a drop of water?

If you counted them you might find there were:
1,237,992,101,573,228,689,214.

The first thing we do is round the number off...
1,240,000,000,000,000,000,000.

Phew! That looks a bit better doesn't it?

Even with the commas, all those zeros are quite confusing, so there is a special way of writing *really* big numbers.

1 Ignore the commas!

2 Write down the digits at the front, in this case 124. Put a decimal point after the first digit, so that you get 1.24.

3 Count the number of digits in your big number and subtract one. In this case there are 22 digits, so $22 - 1 = 21$.

4 You can now write your big number like this:
   1.24×10^{21} (can you see where the 21 goes?).

There! Isn't that easier and neater?

How does 1.24×10^{21} mean 1,240,000,000,000, 000,000,000? What we have done is divide the big number into two new numbers. When you write 10^{21}, this means 10 multiplied by itself 21 times, which is the same as a 1 with 21 zeros after it.

1.24×10^{21} really means 1.24 multiplied by 1,000,000,000,000,000,000,000 which equals 1,240,000,000,000,000,000,000.

Of course, you might have to decode this sort of number too!

Suppose you read that the Earth is 4.65×10^9 years old.

To find out what that means you multiply the sum out ... it's easy! 10^9 is just a 1 with 9 zeros after it so you get $4.65 \times 1,000,000,000$.

The clearest way of multiplying by a number like 1,000,000,000 is to move the decimal point along one place to the right for every zero. In this case there are 9 zeros so move the decimal point *nine* places. You get this:

465_ _ _ _ _ _ _. (After the decimal point moved past the 6 and 5 there were still seven zeros left, so the point moved seven more places.)

Now just fill in the gaps with zeros and you get

4650000000. If you put commas in, then that makes it look tidier and more obvious. You can then say the Earth is 4,650,000,000 years old.

Little calculators and big numbers

When calculators try to show you big numbers, most of them have a special problem. They can't write things like 4.7×10^{13} because they can't do '×'s and they can't do little numbers in the corner. Instead they might put 4.7 E 13.

The number after the letter "E" just tells you how many places to move the decimal point, so for example "E 43" means the same as "$\times 10^{43}$".

If your calculator is really feeble it might just put E without a number. In this case the E stands for *error* – the number is so big your calculator has seized up!

Teeny weeny numbers!

This system that shows massive numbers can also show the tiniest of numbers too.

One atom of hydrogen weighs 1.7×10^{-24} grammes. (Or as a calculator would write it: 1.7 E–24.) Gosh! That looks like a lot until you notice there is a minus sign in front of the 24.

To work out what that looks like, you do exactly the same as you did to find out the age of the Earth … in other words you write down 1.7 then move the decimal point along. However because it is *minus* 24, you move the decimal point the *other way*!

You will find that one atom of hydrogen weighs ... 0.00000000000000000000000017 grammes!

You will realize that the most important thing here is that tiny minus sign. If you missed it out and said that one atom of hydrogen weighed 1.7×10^{24} grammes, then it would be a lot heavier than Mount Everest!

Names of big numbers

Thousand	1,000
Million	1,000,000 (This is the same as a thousand thousand.)
	Just so you know ... if you count steadily it will take you over a week to count to a million – that's if you don't go to sleep first!
Billion	Aha! There's a bit of a problem here. In America it's 1,000,000,000 or a thousand million. However in most places a billion is 1,000,000,000,000 or a million million.
	The good news is that a British billionaire is 1,000 times richer than an American billionaire. The bad news is that there aren't any British billionaires.
	If an American billionaire had all his or her money in $1 bills, it would take him or her 30 years non-stop to count them all!
Trillion	Another problem with America!

	In America this is a million million or 1,000,000,000,000. (The same as our billion.) In most other places it is a million million million or 1,000,000,000,000,000,000 (or 10^{18}).
Zillion	A childish name for any really stupidly big number.
Squillion	A zillion zillions and then a few plonked on top.
Googol	A "1" with 100 zeros after it. You can write it as 10^{100}.
Googolplex	A "1" with a googol zeros after it. WARNING! If you are thinking of writing this one out, you better get everybody else in the whole world to help you.
Infinity	A googolplex of googolplexes hardly breaks the surface here. Infinity is large indeed. At least there's a special sign for it: ∞.

A FINAL WORD ABOUT INFINITY ...

SYMMETRY AND THE MINDMASHING MAZE

Here's a puzzle to think about:
What have these letters got...

A B C D E H I K M O T U V W X Y

... that these haven't?

F G J L N P Q R S Z

You'll be ages thinking about it so here's the answer: the letters in the top line have *reflective symmetry*.

If something has reflective symmetry, that means you can draw a line through the middle of it, and one side is an exact reflection of the other.

Look at this: here you can see one side of the letter A is a reflection of the other.

If you put a mirror on the dotted line and look into it, you will see the shape of a letter "A". If you fold the paper in half, one side of the letter will land exactly on top of the other.

If you were feeling *really* lazy, you could just draw one half of the letter in wet paint, fold the paper over and open it again and the paint that came off on the other side would finish the letter off!

"Hang on!" you exclaim in outrage. "What about the letter 'Z'? You can draw a line through that and one side is a reflection of the other..."

Let's see...

No! The two parts are not reflections, they're the same.

If you tried to make a "Z" the lazy way by painting one half then folding and unfolding the paper, this is what you would get...

Lots of things have reflective symmetry including almost every kind of animal. Your own body will have reflective symmetry unless you have some extra arms on one side or a spare nose growing out of your left kneecap. Or a really wonky haircut.

Some UNsymmetrical animals...

Owls often have one ear opening higher than the other to help them pinpoint animals scuffling in the dark.

Flatfish are fish that swim on their side such as flounder and plaice. They always swim with the same side downwards, but the eye that would be facing downwards has gradually moved round to join the other one on the upperside of the head.

Crabs sometimes have one claw bigger than the other.

Some things have more than one "line" of symmetry. Have a look at the letter "X". You can draw it so that it has *four* possible lines of symmetry!

So you think you know all about symmetry now? OK, how about this then...

What have these letters got...

H I N O S X Z

...that these haven't?

A B C D E F G J K L M P Q R T U V W

The letters on the top line have got *rotational* symmetry! This means that you could pick them up, rotate them and then put them back down on themselves. The best way of seeing how this works is to turn this book round and look at this page upside-down.

SEE HOW THE LETTERS WITH ROTATIONAL SYMMETRY STILL LOOK THE SAME?

Most letters have only two positions of rotational symmetry, but have you noticed there is one letter missing from the list above? Yes, the letter "Y" has been left out because it can be a special case. Normally Y would not have any rotational symmetry, but ... if a Y was drawn carefully with the arms the same length and the angles between the arms all exactly the same, Y would have *three* positions of rotational symmetry!

You will have realized that letters H, I, O and X have both rotational *and* reflective symmetry.

How many positions of rotational symmetry has a cross like the letter "X" got?

How many positions has a circle like the letter "O" got?

Good grief! It looks like you found out about symmetry just in time because you have suddenly been grabbed by Professor Fiendish who has tossed you into his...

Mindmashing maze!
Grugg the gruesome guard will only let you out when you know the magic words to say to him. Start by the door and work your way round the murderous maze writing down the letters as you pass them.

Rules:
1 If you reach a sign with *rotational symmetry*, turn *left*.
2 If you reach a sign with *reflective symmetry*, turn *right*.
3 If you reach a sign with *both types*, you must double back.
4 If you reach a sign with *no symmetry*, go straight on.
5 By the time you get back to the door you should know the magic words. Say them nicely!

DOOR

(Hint: Your first two letters should be 'y' and 'o')

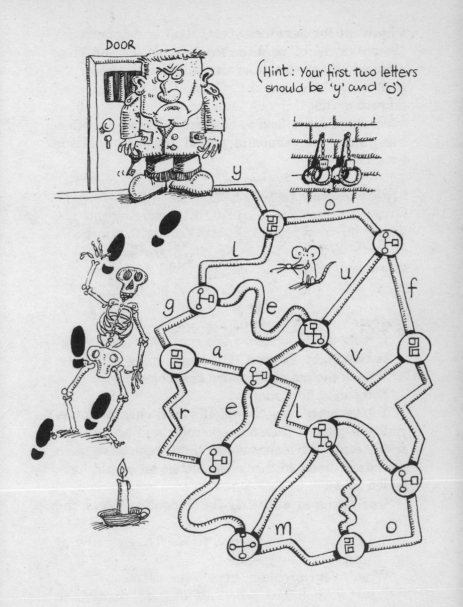

y

o

l

u

f

g

e

a

v

r

e

l

m

o

141

Payment for services

"You're my hero!" said the Princess as she and Thag stepped off the bottom of the ladder.

"I must confess, the Colonel is paying me," admitted Thag.

"Well, he can afford to because my father is offering him a one thousand pound reward!" said the Princess.

"Is that right, Colonel? Oh dear!" sniggered Thag.

"What's the matter?" asked the Colonel.

"You can't afford me!"

"You've been very cheap! If I had chosen to pay you one pound, then two pounds and so on, this seventeenth payment would have been seventeen pounds. I dread to think what that lot would have added up to."

"One hundred and fifty-three pounds," said the Princess.

The Princess looked round to see Thag staring at her in rapture.

"What's your problem, hero?" she asked.

"I just love a girl who can deal in digits," he stammered.

"Well, I'm just very glad I'm not paying you one hundred and fifty-three pounds," said the Colonel.

"So how much is he paying you?" asked the Princess.

"One penny for the first job, tuppence for the second, four pence for the third, and it keeps doubling," said Thag.

"Pennies!" scoffed the Colonel.

"Did you say there were seventeen payments?" asked the Princess.

"Yes," said Thag.

"Boy!" gushed the Princess. "You're quite a number rumbler yourself!"

"Don't be too impressed," said the Colonel. "He turned down fifty pounds instead of his seventeenth payment!"

"I'll say he did!" gasped the Princess. "Does the Colonel know what the seventeenth payment is?"

"Not yet," admitted Thag.

The Colonel looked worried. "It's only pennies, surely," he said.

"Sixty-five thousand, five hundred and thirty-six of them," said the Princess.

"Sixty-five thousand..." began the Colonel.

"Or if you prefer, six hundred and fifty-five pounds, and thirty-six pence," said Thag.

"And that's just the seventeenth payment," said the Princess.

"How ... how much is the total?" asked the Colonel.

"One thousand, three hundred and ten pounds," said the Princess.

"And seventy-one pence," said Thag.

"Boy oh boy," the Princess gushed, "that's everything I like in a man. Bravado, brains and loose change."

A few weeks later the Valiant Vector Warriors were forming the guard of honour as Thag and the new Mrs Princess Thag walked by covered in confetti.

"Hooray," cheered all the Warriors.

"I trust you'll all be coming to the wedding feast," said Thag.

"We've got loads of cold sausages for you," said the Princess. "Seven hundred and twenty-eight of them to be exact."

"Hooray even more," cheered the Warriors.

"How many sausages each is that?" asked the Colonel.

"Are you asking me?" laughed Thag. "Because it'll cost you another payment."

The Colonel went very pale. "Maybe I'll just have a bit of cake instead," he said.